MW01615797

Jackie Johnson
923 Wadey Drive
Regina, Saskatchewan
Canada S4N 7G9

ISBN 0-9732654-0-X

Printed and bound in Canada by
Print 1 Instant Services Ltd.
2125 15th Avenue
Regina, Saskatchewan
Canada
www.print1regina.com

Pam you only fail if you don't try

Jackie Jo

To obtain copies of this book, contact Jackie Johnson at the above address or visit:

www.trickhorse.ca
OR
www.stunthorse.com

1

Every once in a while, someone will say something with such great meaning that I carry it with me for the rest of my life. I think it only fitting that I pass these words of wisdom along. "Thank you," to everyone who made me who I am today:

"The last thing that you let go of is the reins"
~Chuck McIlwrick

The first and perhaps the best riding lesson that I ever got was from my dad and it consisted of this simple instruction before I was sent on my way to make my mistakes, achieve my successes and learn my lessons – both good and bad.

"Eat something so your head is clear"
~ Gail McIlwrick

Don't bother trying to teach on an empty stomach, and don't expect your horse to try and learn on an empty stomach. Everyone and everything become irritable when they are hungry.

"Don't worry about what others think, just worry about yourself"
~ Rod Johnson

If you spend enough time with horses, you will soon find yourself open to scrutiny on the methods that you use. My husband, with these 10 simple words, quickly puts things into perspective for me every time.

"You spent a lot of money filling your head with knowledge now, protect it"
~ Dr. Joann McIlwrick
~ Dr. Cory Toth

Don't let pride cloud your judgment. Wear a helmet. Another famous sister and brother-in-law quote, "You think that you'll look silly wearning a helmet? You'll look a lot sillier in a spine stabilizing halo."

"Because you can't fail if you don't try"
~ Brenda Sapergia

When asked why everyone doesn't train his/her horse to perform stunts

"It is easy to say 'do it' but one must always explain 'why'."
~ John Knubben

My dear friend and accomplished horseman. Throughout this book, I have done my best to explain '"Why"..

A couple of more "Thank yous" are also in order:

Thank you, Mom and Dad for your loving support, direction and willingness to build strange contraptions like pedestals, portable corral panels, and branding irons.

Thank you, to my loving, wonderful, husband, Rod. You never complain when I spend more time at the farm than I do at home.

To Brenda Sapergia - Thank you, for putting up with me, for what has become, a few years. Without your direction, advice, sense of adventure, and picture taking abilities, I would never have been able to compile this book.

To John Wood - Who took me out horse buying when I decided I was ready to purchase a horse of my own all those years ago.

To Jackie and Robert Moser, and their two sons, Adam and Darren - The J over R brand on the hip of Cash and Reamo is from their farm. Jackie and Bob have an exquisite eye for both beauty and brains in horses, and her 2 boys are phenominal in the work that they do starting colts for resale. I would never hesitate to buy, over the phone, a horse from Jackie (1-306-957-2067)

In memory of, and thank you to, my Uncle Wally Maier, who was always a phone call away when I had any questions about feed and health.

Thank you, again, to my family. I can't thank you enough for all that you have done for me.

And Thank you, God, for putting this path at my feet for me to follow.

One of the most difficult tasks of compiling this book was finding the photos that captured "That Moment". The photos within are captured over the years, and by a variety of devices. Some are scanned in, some are taken with a digital camera, but most are captured off video. It is for this reason that some of the photos might be grainy. In an effort to present a realistic training picture, I, toward the end of the book, found myself, in frigid winter temperatures, hustling out to find an untrained horse. Just as you can't learn to drive by standing on the sidewalk watching vehicles pass, you can't learn to train trick horses by watching a finished horse perform. Photos of "Duster" (Bonnington Farms Cherokee Knight) are perfect examples of this. These illustrations aren't the greatest, but it is impossible to re-create the clumsiness with which a horse searches for a

Pico the Donkey lies down for a local daycare demonstration

pedestal when learning to step onto it. To show photos of Duster stepping on his ped now would be showing photos of a trained horse rather than one 'in training'. This is also true of photos of him bowing. In many cases, re-doing the session looses the nitty gritty of the training steps, so I have decided to present the photos that capture the training moments as they appear. They are without frills, fancy backgrounds, or proper lighting. This is trick training as it really happens.

Reamo resting before a fundraising event while temperatures climbed to 107 degrees.

INTRODUCTION

This book is intended to be an owner's manual for the Trick Horse - and if you think about it, wouldn't it be great if all horses came with an owner's manual? Time and time again, the question/comment arises, "You'd better think about how long you intend to keep that horse before you teach him those things!" And this is a very serious question to consider before embarking down the trick-training road. A trick horse is not your typical horse! He is trained to perform amazing feats and, without an operator's guide, everyone runs the risk of being seriously injured. Worst of all, the horse runs the risk of being mis-understood and mislabelled should he fall into the hands of someone unfamilliar with his knowledge. So, throw this book in your glove box, or in with your horse's papers and vet records. It is not intended to sit on your shelf and collect dust.

Once training has started, it is meant to accompany your horse for the rest of his life.

Now, before we get into the nitty-gritty, there are some things that you have to consider about this book, and trick training in general. With your horse in mind, this book is set up backwards. Each section first explains the finished trick, and the cues to achieve that trick. Then I provide detailed instruction on how to get there. There are two reasons for this presentation. First, it is much easier to understand the path if you can see your destination. When you first start trick training your horse, you will be rewarding the horse's "try" – which could be as subtle as his lean or a shift in his weight. Second, so that if you, or people new to your horse's life, ever need to find a trained cue, the answer is right at hand and not buried deep in a lot of text. With your horse in mind, please do not sit down and read this book cover to cover, and then run to run out to the barn and expect to train him everything in one weekend! In order to have a finished trick horse, you must be prepared to invest hours, weeks, months, and years. When training trick horses, it is pretty easy to get lost in the big picture and lose confidence in yourself and your training abilities. By taking things one step at a time, you will find more success and less frustration – I promise!

Another aspect of this book that you must consider is that it is just one person's opinion (mine!) on how to train trick horses. There are MANY different ways to achieve a trick – from a complete use of riggings, to clickers to the complete absence of ropes. In the ten years that I have been training trick horses I have tried many of the methods out there (and some I have tried just once!). You must understand that there is no right or wrong method to training trick horses. There are effective methods, and ineffective ones - mine is certainly not the only method and in some cases, you might find what I do is incompatible with you, your circumstances and your horse. Everyone has a different comfort level, and everyone is at a different level in his horse and training experience. You must have confidence in your OWN knowledge and experience. Trust that you and your horse can do this together. Trick training is all about communication and trust. You and your horse will communicate with each other until you both develop the mutual trust and respect necessary to perform the trick. As you and your horse become more comfortable with each other (and more confident in each other), you will come up with different training ideas until you develop your own style. I can provide you with the direction, but it is up to you and your horse to develop the fine-tuning.

WHY DO YOU WANT TO TRICK TRAIN YOUR HORSE?

Well…why DO you want to train your horse to do this stuff? You should really think about it because it's always handy to have an answer on hand when some grumpy old guy, who is really set in his ways, asks: "Why the heck would you want to teach your horse to do that?!"

It has always been my nature to train my horses beyond the everyday, normal (boring), tasks. Where I'm from it gets pretty cold in the winter (minus 30 degrees Celsius) and unless you don't mind walking a wet horse around until 1:00 in the morning…you find things to do with him that don't involve a lot of sweat! So, I spend my time teaching tricks during the winter, as a break from the physical demands that I place on my horse during the summer months. Initially, the tricks were a novelty at which people could chuckle and shake their heads, but they also started to develop purpose. If a trick horse somehow gets his foot caught in something (like the bottom wire on the fence) chances are he is going to wait for you to come and get him out of it. If you don't happen to be handy, then he might possibly think his way out of it rather than panic and cut himself up. If something scary is coming towards a trick horse, you can tell him to "hold" and "stand" (two words that you are going to rely on quite a bit when you start trick training). The horse will know that, while whatever is coming towards him might be pretty freaky, you won't let anything bad happen to him.

Some other times when trick training has come in quite handy: If you have just walked to the farthest pasture to get your horse and you don't feel like walking all the way home, ask your horse to bow for an easy boost onto his back. If you ride in an area where people are inconsiderate (around here folks don't slow down when passing horses, and I have also been dive bombed by model airplanes when riding) ask your trick horse for a "rear-up" to 'pretend' that you are 'out of control'…. You'd be surprised how fast people slow down for you when they think that you might damage their car! If your horse is feeling his oats, ask him to "march" to get his focus back on you. People who don't have trained trick horses generally ask their horses to "back up" to regain control, but I have seen some pretty hairy "back-ups" into ditches, fences and bushes. Asking your horse to "march" lets him blow off some steam and puts you back in control. The "lie-down" is very handy if you would like to check for and remove ticks from your horses belly. I also use the "lie down" to brush winter hair from bellys, inspect sheaths, doctor belly or leg scrapes, and administer fly spray in otherwise hard to reach areas.

The benefits of training your horse to do tricks are endless. Don't be fooled though, there are also some things that will leave you shaking your head. Lots of trick horses learn to unlatch their pen gates, climb fences, or any number of things. I have found my trick horse standing on top of a covered water trough and even though I never taught him how to untie himself, he always manages to get free from where I've tied him. I have dealt with a trick horse that always managed to escape his fenced enclosure and get into his favorite pasture night after night, although I never did see how he did it. I have also had trick horses crawl under the fence for a drink from a preferred water source, then crawl back under again to get back with their buddies. So, when you train your horse tricks you also need to have a good sense of humor. It will help you get your horse off the water trough, and it will also help you explain to the owner of said water trough just how those hoof prints managed to get up there.

SOME VERY IMPORTANT THINGS

Even though your horse might not intend to hurt you, trick training is similar to horses roughhousing with their pasture friends. In the spirit of the game, your horse might forget that you aren't a pasture buddy and deliver a playful blow or nip. When you first start trick training, your horse will be off balance. Teaching the bow and rear, for example, put the two of you into a precarious position. The danger of your horse falling on top of you is very real!! If you don't believe that training a trick horse is dangerous, then this is just not for you. Accidents and mistakes happen all the time and the best defense is a good offence. Part of that offence involves two of the most important requirements - horse preparation and ground preparation.

First, you must have a horse with **exceptional** ground manners, and second you must have the proper ground. If your horse isn't ready, you don't need to bother looking for the proper ground, so let's start with the horse. Choose the scenario that best describes you and your horse:

A quick bow, and I'm able to easily get onto Reamo's back during a trick clinic. The bow can be a lazy man's mounting block!

A. *You grab the halter and walk out to the pasture to catch your horse. As you are walking toward him, he sees you and starts to walk to you, pausing occasionally to munch on the fresh grass. After a polite "hello" and a quick scratch behind his ears, you quietly slip the halter over his nose, his ears, and fasten the buckle. As you turn toward the barn, your horse falls in beside you to follow on a loose lead. You tie him in the barn, where he stands, quietly munching the oats that you have waiting for him. Grabbing the hoof-pick, you ask him for his front foot. He shifts his weight so that you can pick up his foot, and he stands while you thoroughly clean his hoof. As you finish with that hoof, he shifts his weight and cocks the next foot waiting for you to pick it up. After you finish cleaning his hooves, you tug on his nostrils and look in his mouth to see if his wolf teeth have come in yet. You also feel inside his ears for any bugs or abrasions. Throughout the whole thing, your horse stands quietly, as he is quite used to this.*

B. *You grab the halter and walk out to the pasture to catch your horse. As you are walking toward him, he sees you and starts to amble the other way. You shake the oat bucket, hoping to catch his attention. Tempted by the oats, he comes to you, and while he dips his head into the bucket you quickly reach out and grab onto his mane before he takes off. Startled, he tries to get away but you hang on until he realizes that he is caught. You push the halter over his nose and quickly stuff his ears through as he shakes his head in agitation. On the way to the barn, you walk at your horses shoulder as he dances and tugs on the rope, dragging you along. You tie him in the barn where he immediately starts to fidget and dance, shoving you aside to get to his oats. Grabbing the hoof pick and his fetlock with both hands, you wrestle his front foot off the ground and do a quick pick before he puts it back down again. Carefully, you wrestle his back foot off the ground, holding on as he does a few quick jerks and mini kicks. You see his hoof isn't that dirty just before he jerks it out of your hands and puts it back on the ground. The only time you handle his mouth is when you stick your fingers in there to get the bit in and he really tosses his head when you try to touch his ears.*

So, which scenario are you? Before you can train a trick horse, you have to be able to handle his ears (inside and out), handle his muzzle, and pick up each foot, letting it down only when YOU decide that you are done with it. If you are scenario "A", then keep reading, your horse is ready for trick training. If you are scenario "B", then you MUST establish a more dominant role in the relationship that you have with your horse BEFORE you can start trick training. This means that you can catch, halter, and lead, your horse without incident. This means that you can safely and consistently pick up your horse's feet, and this means that you can handle his ears and muzzle - ALL without incident. Without strong direction and control, and consistent discipline, a trick horse can become a dangerous and unpredictable animal. If you are scenario "B", then put this book down and go develop the relationship that you need to have with your horse. He needs to respect you before you start trick training.

Now that we have determined whether or not your horse is ready, it's time to look at the ground requirements. For tricks involving the bow, kneel, lie-down and sit-up, you MUST have deep, soft, ground. We don't all have access to deep sand arenas or specially prepared areas, but there are many good alternatives.

Cash is lying in a thick bed of sand.

12

If you don't have ideal ground conditions, make the best of it by wrapping legs and knees with cushioning wraps. In this case, I have taken my skid boots and turned them upside down to cover Reamo's knees. You don't need fancy wraps! Polo wraps, and even slightly modified kneepads from your volleyball or rollerblading days will work just as well.

If you don't have access to a soft arena, then ask yourself this question: "If I got bucked off my horse today, where (on the ground) would I want to land?". You might choose the nearby sand pit, a freshly worked field, or the straw bale stack with all the loose straw and broken bales. Regardless of how soft your training area, remember that it is always good practice to put protective padding on your horse's legs and particularly on his knees. If your horse starts to scrape his knees during a bow because the ground is abrasive, then he will become very reluctant to perform the bow and kneel. Likewise, if the ground is not soft enough for the lie-down, you will not be able to successfully train this trick. Soft ground is imperative for trick training.

LET'S GET STARTED

First of all, you will notice that I refer to the horse as "he". This doesn't mean that you can only trick train geldings or studs, it just means that it was a lot quicker to type "he" than it was to type" she". There are absolutely NO restrictions or limitations when it comes to trick horses, or trick donkeys, trick mini's, trick ponies, or trick mules, for that matter. From newborn to senior, you can trick train any age, size, make or model of horse and his cousins as long as you are prepared to spend the time. When training a trick horse, the optimal amount of time to spend with one horse is 35 to 40 HOURS a week. Obviously this just isn't feasible for a lot of people. If you want to have a safe, consistent, well-rounded trick horse, and if you want to see results, then you MUST invest the time. If you can only spend weekends and holidays with your horse, then trick training may not be for you. When your time is limited, it isn't fair to expect your horse to learn advanced tricks like the bow, lie-down, sit up, and rear. An alternative would be to choose simple tricks like hugs and kisses or yes and no. When it comes to training trick horses, there is no mystery! If you spend the time with your horse, you can do ANYTHING!

So where do you start? I used to say that there was a recommended sequence for trick training. I have realized that I don't follow that rule, so I might as well quit telling other people to follow it! Oh sure, it's true that you can't get to the sit -up without going through the bow and lie-down, but, the fact of the matter is, you start where your horse tells you to start. If your horse is constantly picking up buckets and brushes and likes to rip the posters off the wall of the barn, or if you always seem to find your horse's halter and rope in the field or in his stall - then you have a very oral horse and you should probably consider starting with "Smile" and "Take It" which focus on his head and mouth. If your horse paws when he's tied, paws against the side of his stall, paws against the wall of your trailer, or somehow always seems to get his foot caught in fences, then you should start with teaching the march, pedestal work, salute, and count. When trick training, work with your horse to control his naturally occurring actions, then you can communicate when you would like those actions to be performed. Not only does this keep your horse happy (because he can still do the things that come naturally to him), but it also gives you grounds for discipline when he performs these actions without your request (like pawing up the inside of your new trailer). So take the time to have a good, long visit, with your horse. When he tells you what he'd like to do, then it's time to start trick training.

Investigating the taste of a shirt that was left behind, Spike tells me that he might be good at picking things up with his mouth.

15

One last thing before we get started. When training trick horses I prefer to use a food reward. I use a 16% horse crunch, which is a cube-type bulk feed that sells for $11.00 for a 40lb bag. If you decide to use food as your training reward, you don't have to spend a lot of money and you don't have to travel far and wide. Talk to your feed supply store and see if they have cubed horse feed. Carrots are great to use, if your horse likes them because they can be broken into small pieces. Oats work well too, but you have to watch that your fingers don't accidentally get nipped. You don't have to use a food reward! Praise, clickers, targets, or whatever other method of reward is on the market today work great. As you teach your horse more and more, you will build a strong communication channel and develop your own training methods and ideas. Remember that the secret to training a trick horse is in the constructive time spent, not necessarily in the training method.

When possible, buy your treats in bulk. You will go through a lot of them!

Enough dry theory, let's get started!!
SECTION I

TRICKS USING THE HEAD

I am frequently asked, "How long will it take me to teach my horse to…?" That's kind of like asking, "How long is a piece of string?" - the answer is almost impossible. How much time you already spend with your horse, the communication between the two of you, the style of training that you choose, your horses capacity to learn, and your ability to teach, are all factors. The time duration also depends upon how much finesse you want on your trick. You can teach a horse to bow by wrestling him into the ground in fewer than three hours, but it takes significantly longer to make it look pretty. Finally, just when you think that you have everything working well, someone will come along and tell you that you aren't that great because you can't work at liberty. Chin up though! Trick Training is a life long process.

HUG

Requirements: Treat reward
Watch Out For: Nipped fingers if you are using a treat reward.

You have to be a little flexible to start this trick but when you have finished training, here is how the hug will work.

Stand close to your horse on his left side facing his shoulder. With your left hand, reach under his neck, this placing the palm of your left hand on the right side of his neck. Press lightly on his neck where your palm is resting and tell your horse to, "Give me a hug."

Your horse will wrap his head and neck around your body in a horsey hug. Tap his girth to let him know that the hug is finished and he will unwrap his neck. Give him his reward. He has done well!

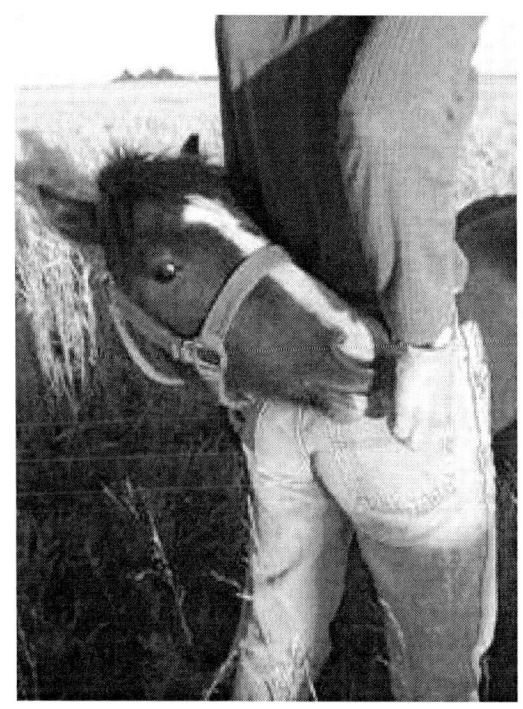

With a piece of bait, I am encouraging Spike, the pony, to wrap his head and neck around my body in a horse style hug.

Even though Spike is small, I am using my hand on his neck (above it because he is small) to start building a cue for the hug.

Now that you know what you are trying to achieve, let's break down the steps. First, find an area with minimal distractions. Stand close to your horse on the left side facing his shoulder. With your left hand, reach under his neck, this placing the palm of your hand on the right side of his neck. Press lightly on his neck where your palm is resting and tell your horse to, "Give me a hug." At the same time that you are doing this, reach behind your back with your right hand (you should be holding the treat reward) and turn slightly to show your horse that you are holding his treat behind you. As your horse reaches for the treat, he will wrap his head and neck around you. Give him his reward and tap his girth or provide some other cue to signal that the trick is over.

We give the horse his reward before we signal the end of the trick until he begins to understand that he wraps his head and neck around you when you give him the cue. Repeat the hug request. As your horse begins to understand where his reward is, twist less and have him reach further before giving the reward and tapping his girth to signal the end of the trick. Your horse will soon realize that when you cue him on the neck and ask for a hug there will be a reward waiting on the other side of you. When he gets to this point, withhold the reward and signal the end of the trick by tapping his girth Then step away and give him his treat reward for a job well done.

We switch the treat reward with the end of trick cue so that the hug becomes a learned behavior rather than a response generated by food. This will minimize the potential for complete food dependency and ensure that you build a solid trick should you find yourself showing your stuff without treats on hand. If your horse is somewhat distracted, or if he starts to deliver his hugs less than 100%, you can remind him of his job by reaching behind your back during the hug cue and snapping your fingers to bring his head all the way around.

Treats and rewards are payment for a job well done. In the beginning, there is nothing wrong with using a lot of treats but your horse should remember that treats are earned, not owed. As a trainer, you are responsible for issuing payment so ensure that you don't needlessly reward lackluster attempts.

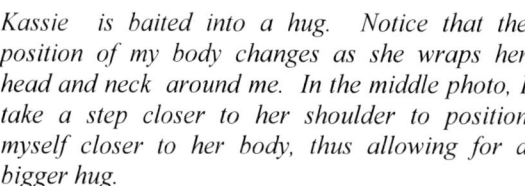

Kassie is baited into a hug. Notice that the position of my body changes as she wraps her head and neck around me. In the middle photo, I take a step closer to her shoulder to position myself closer to her body, thus allowing for a bigger hug.

KISS

Requirements: Treat Reward
Watch Out For: An over eager horse nipping your face or hitting you in the face with his nose.

Standing in front of your horse, lean forward slightly and ask your horse to give you a kiss. Your horse will touch your lips with his nose. Make a kissy noise to indicate that the trick has been completed.

Teaching the kiss is just like teaching a horse how to touch a target – in this case, the target is going to be your lips. Tease your horse with a cookie to show him that you have a treat reward for him. Hold the food reward up near your cheek and ask your horse for a kiss. When he reaches for the treat, touch his nose with your lips, make a kissing noise and give him his reward. Keep practicing in this way so that your horse learns to raise his head to you when you lean forward and ask for the kiss.

After showing Sally where the cookie is, I draw her nose to my lips while saying "Give me a kiss!". I lean forward slightly to complete the kiss and give a kissy, squeaking, noise to let Sally know that the trick has been completed. After practicing, I will be able to lower my hand, lean forward and ask for a kiss. From t h e b o d y language of leaning forward, plus the verbal request, Sally will give me a great big horsey smooch.

A seasoned kisser. Reamo puckers up when I lean forward.

When your horse starts to understand the kiss request, start to drop your hand from your face – a good place to put it is behind your back so that your horse doesn't start to pester your hand for the treat. Your horse will remember that the last place he got his treat was up at your face and he will start to move his nose toward you. Reward his first, fumbling attempts, as long as he is raising his head upward then he is trying. Soon, your horse will have it figured out that if he touches his nose to your lips, he will get a treat. Don't forget to kiss at him each time to mark the end of the trick.

As I mentioned in the "Watch Out For" section, be careful that your over-eager horse doesn't try to nip you in the face. Watch for the first signs that he is going to start using his mouth, such as reaching with his lips. Your horse shouldn't have to reach with his lips for this trick, all he should do is touch his nose to your face.

Sometimes you just have to appreciate that horses have a sense of humor. Reamo 'laughs' at my request for a kiss, opting instead, for a big toothy grin. This is where 'knowing your horse' is the key. In this case, I know that Reamo is smiling at me, but when requesting the kiss, always be aware of exactly what your horse is doing. While I have never (yet) had a horse try to bite me while offering the kiss, there is a first time for everything. The most common kiss related mishaps are when the horse swings his head up too fast and bumps you in the face harder than expected. As with any other trick, control is the key and rude kisses should be reprimanded rather than rewarded.

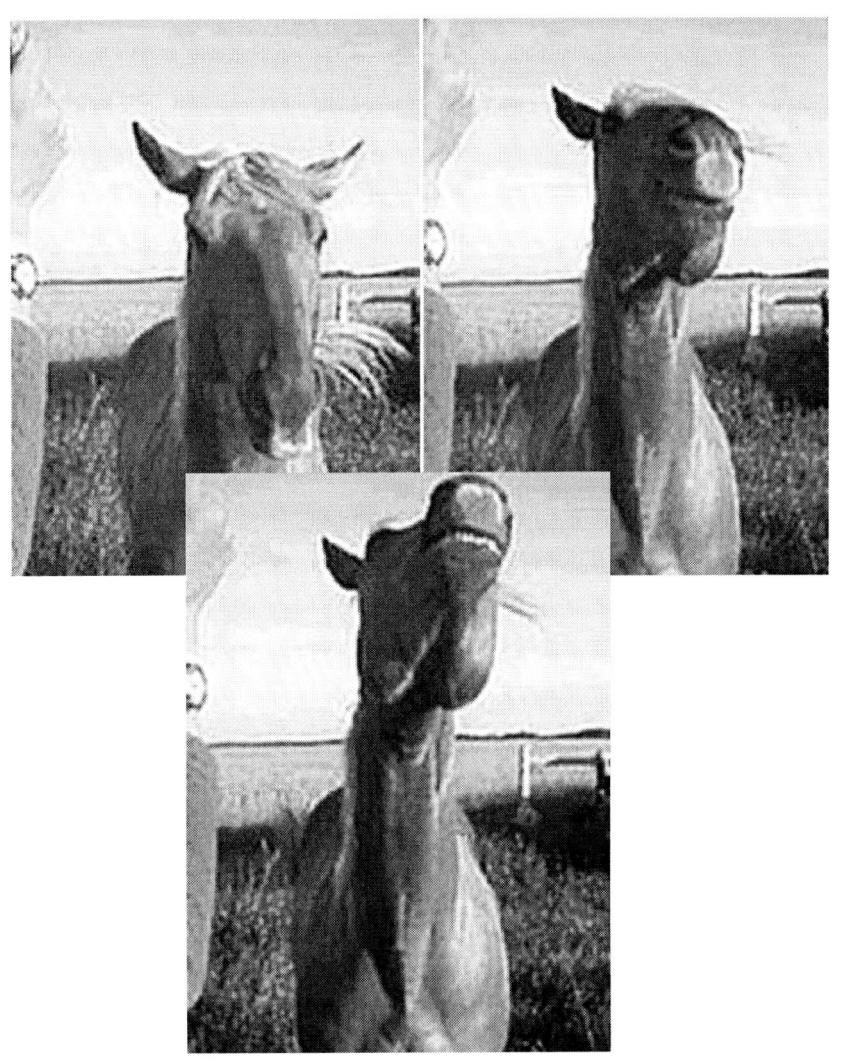

You can see my hand at the left cueing Reamo to nod yes.

YES

Requirements: Large halter, treat reward.

Stand in front of your horse, hold a treat at your shoulder level and ask, "Do you want a cookie?" Your horse will nod his head, "Yes."

Set the halter to the largest size and drop the nose band down over top of the horse's nose (just above his nostrils). Your horse will find this annoying and flip his head to get the halter off his nostrils and back up on the bridge of his nose where it belongs.

Stand in front of your horse, slide the halter down on to his nose, then quickly raise the food reward and ask, "Do you want a cookie?" Two things become the cue, your raised hand, and the tone of your voice – don't forget, you ARE asking a question. When he flips the halter off his nose, give him his treat and tell him he is a good boy. You want to get him to associate your raised hand with flipping his head rather than with the halter over his nose. After you have practiced the halter, hand, voice sequence, start to eliminate the halter over his nose by switching the sequence to: show the cookie, then ask the question. If you don't get a response, THEN reach out with your other hand and pull the halter over his nose.

As soon as he flips his head, drop your hand and give him his reward. Keep practicing this until your horse is able to flip his head without you using the backup cue of pulling the halter over his nose. Don't forget to reward 'try'. You don't have to provide a food reward for lackluster performance, but you must encourage your horse if he tries to go in the right direction. This might mean that he just raises his head slightly…but as long as he is trying at the beginning of teaching this trick, then reward him as if he has done it perfectly.

At the start, don't worry if your horse only gives one nod. As you practice, you can teach him that as long as your hand is up, he should be nodding his head. You can reinforce multiple nods by pulling his halter down over his nose until he gives you three or four nods in sequence. The more you practice, the less you will have to rely on the halter.

A method used by others involves a sharp object that will mimic

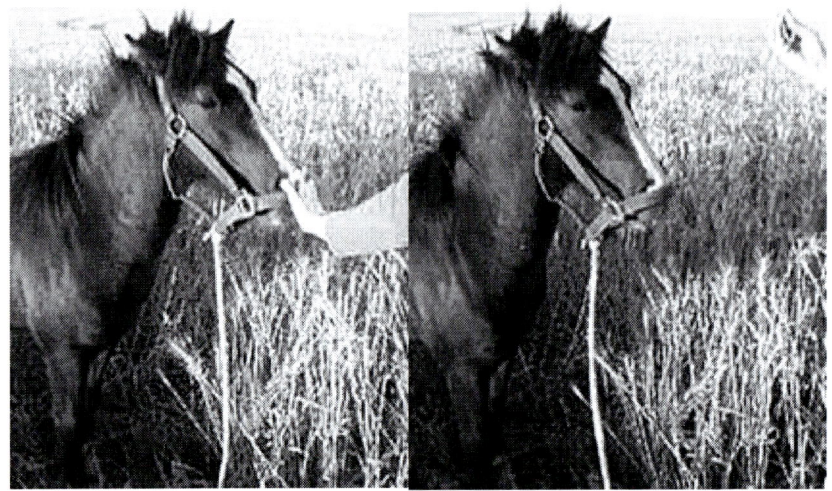

Pulling an oversized halter down over the nose of your horse will cause him to flip his head in a "yes" style. With the help of the halter, you can condition him to nod his head up and down.

a fly bite. You can tell when horses have been taught this way because the handler will stand at the shoulder facing forward. The handler will touch the mane at the base of his neck, just in front of the withers and the horse will nod his head yes or no, depending upon how they respond to the sharp irritant. Although this is an effective method of training, it isn't the method that I prefer because, however mild, the horse responds to pain rather than a learned behavior. Whenever I see this trick performed this way, I am reminded of the James Harriott story of when he is trying to measure ponies for a show. He was unable to measure one pony because every time the stick touched its withers, the pony would sink down making an accurate measurement impossible. It was discovered that the pony had been pricked in the withers with pins and nails to the point that it sank whenever anything touched its withers. Another reason I prefer my method over the use of a sharp object is, if you would ever like to perform your tricks at liberty, from a distance, my method already puts the "Yes" cue in the air, off the horse.

In this photo sequence, you can see how Spike flips the halter up and off his nose. Just out of photo range, I am holding my hand up to establish a cue. The rope attached to the halter serves no purpose, it is just lying on the ground. Not yet familliar with the new trick, you can see that Spike is offering 'the next best thing' - a salute.

So, in case you haven't figured it out already, the way some folks teach the nod or headshake "no," is by poking the horse just in front of the withers or on the chest and he will start to nod his head in a "yes" or "no" fashion which is a natural horse response to an irritant of this nature. At this point, asking a question becomes pointless because the horse is responding to the discomfort rather than a verbal cue. However, the decision is yours when it comes to training this trick.

Ok! Now that I have frowned upon horses responding to discomfort rather than cues, continue on to the 'Shake No', where we will teach our horse to... respond to discomfort rather than a cue.

A very animated NO! You can see that I am cueing at the left.

NO

Requirements:　　Treat reward
Watch Out For: There is no way that you can train this trick if your horse is at all head shy!　You MUST have a horse whose ears you can handle inside and out before you start this trick.

Stand in front of your horse, point at him with your left index finger, and ask him a question requiring a 'no' response.　It doesn't really matter what the question is, because the real cue here is the pointing of your index finger.　Your horse will shake his head 'No'.　You are going to be sticking your finger in his ear so that it tickles and causes him to shake his head.　You only need to put your finger in his ear just enough for him to shake his head.　There is no danger to his eardrum, as you won't be sticking your finger in that deep!

Stand facing your horse, point at him with your left index finger, and ask him a question requiring a 'no' response.　Of course, your horse won't know what you are asking, so reach up and stick your finger into his right ear.　He will immediately shake his head. Give him his treat and tell him that he is a good boy! You will only have to stick your finger in his ear a few times before he will get to know that it is coming. Point your finger and ask your question. If your horse doesn't respond, move your finger up toward his ear and he will shake his head before you get a chance to stick your finger in his ear. More practice and soon you won't even have to move your finger toward his ear. Don't forget to give him his treats and tell him what a good boy he is.

Although very difficult to capture, this photo illustrates me tickling the hair inside of Reamo's ear to reinforce the headshake 'No'

In this case, the treat is more of an apology for being such a 'pain in the ear' and not a reward for a learned action. In the nod, for example, the horse is instantly rewarded. The head flip removes the annoying halter from his nose, and he gets a food reward to boot! In the "shake no," your horse either responds to the finger cue or he gets a tickle in his ear. The treat afterwards is incidental.

If you don't feel comfortable sticking your finger in your horse's ear, you can also tickle his ear with a piece of thick string a feather or whatever else is handy. The only reason that I prefer using my finger is because I always know where it is.
Important Notes: If you notice that your horse is really trying to

evade your finger moving toward his ear, then just ask for one more head shake and end the training session for the day, or for a little while. If your horse tries to evade your finger rather than shake his head, then he isn't associating your finger with the head-shake and he needs some time to gather his thoughts. It is also important that you end each session by handling your horses ears inside and out until the trick is learned. Show your horse that every time you reach toward his ears it doesn't mean that you are going to annoy him. To avoid a head shy horse, you must desensitize the ears after every session of 'no' training until the trick is learned.

Rather than responding with a head-shake, Kassie turns her head away in an attempt to avoid my tickling her ear. It's time to stop training for a while. Take a short walk around to let your horse gather his thoughts before returning to train the "No." You can see that I don't have my finger that far in Kassies' ear, rather I am tickling her ear by running my finger lightly along the hair within.

A smile with a hand cue, and at liberty. As you practice the smile, you can decrease your horse's dependency on you and move your cue to the air. You can see that the liberty smile doesn't have as much animation as the one with the hand cue. If you are performing a liberty smile and your horse doesn't respond, you always have the hand cue for backup.

SMILE

Requirements: Treat reward, halter.

Standing on the right side of your horse, beside his head and facing forward, ask him for a big smile. At the same time that you are asking, put your finger under his chin. Your horse will lift his top lip in a big toothy grin.

We have all seen our horses do this. They get a whiff of something and raise their top lips to get a better idea of what it is they just smelled. In light of knowing this, please do not try to mimic the effect by putting ammonia, bleach, vinegar or any other strong smelling substance under his nose. Not only is this an unsafe, and unhealthy idea, but it won't work!!

To teach the smile, stand on the right side of your horse, beside his head, facing forward. Put the fingers of your left hand under his chin where you will be able to feel the jawbones that make a "V". Put your fingers into this "V," which is where your cue is going to be placed. The reason that you put your fingers into the 'V' of the jaw is so that you can control the placement of his head which allows you to 'point' the smile in whatever direction you wish.

Now that you have control of his head, tease him with your treat reward. Tickle his nose with it and hold it just out of his reach. The goal is to get your horse to reach for the treat with his lips. Rather than hold the treat out, hold it up so that it encourages him to reach out with his top lip. As soon as your horse makes even the smallest attempt to reach for the treat with his lip, reward him with the treat and tell him what a good boy he is! As you practice, his lip will reach further and further until it is completely extended.

Once your horse is reaching fully for the treat, time to eliminate it! Wean him off the treat by asking him for the smile (remember that the cue is under his chin now). If he doesn't produce the smile, then bring the reward up for him to reach.

Once he smiles, give him his reward. Repeat, but if he still relies on the treat being raised, instead of giving him the treat reward, just tell him that he is a good boy. He will have to work a bit harder to get the actual treat! The goal is to raise your hand a shorter and shorter distance until your horse smiles without you having to raise your hand at all! Don't forget, when you are weaning him off the treat cue, you have to reward 'try'. It's almost like going back to the beginning of teaching the trick but the learning curve is much steeper.

This smile sequence, taken from video shows Spike learning to smile. My hand under his chin acts as both a cue and a guide. In the last photo, Spike is learning to smile from the cue under his chin and relies less on my bait hand.

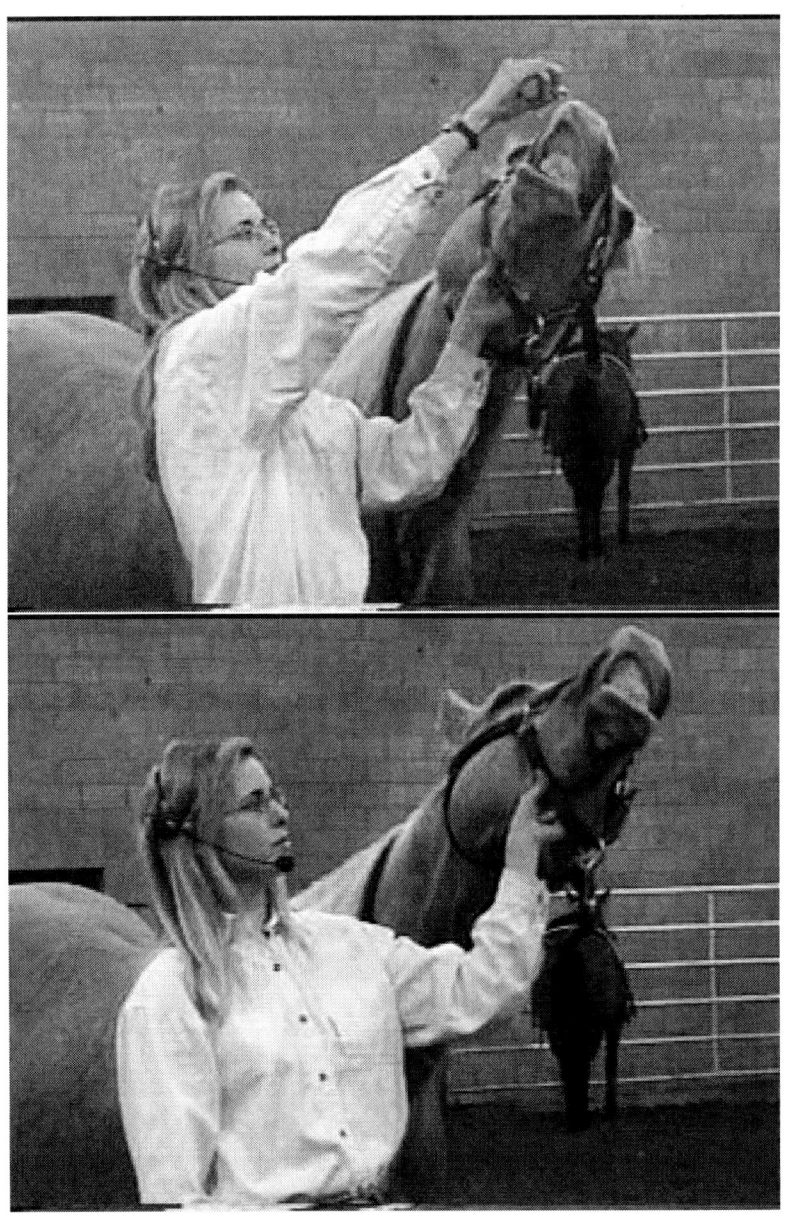

Once your horse learns to smile it's time to wean him off the treats by cueing this trick under the chin only.

TAKE IT

Requirements: Treat Reward, something that your horse likes to pick up.

Watch Out For: When you teach your horse to pick things up, expect that he is now going to pick everything up! Although you shouldn't tolerate a bratty horse (and everyone has their own level of tolerance when it comes to determining what a brat is), you will have to appreciate when he picks up his brushes, buckets and whatever else is within reach. It is OK to punish the behavior, but just remember that YOU taught it, so punish judiciously.

Point to your brush lying on the ground and command, "Take It!" Your horse walks over to the brush, picks it up and brings it back to you to exchange it for a treat reward. You take the brush and ask him to "Release it", your horse lets go and you give him his treat.

Training "Take It!" is a real test of the communication that you have with your horse. There is no way that you can forcibly put something into a horse's mouth and have him keep it there of his own free will. This is definitely a trick where the horse chooses to participate. In light of this fact, you, as the trainer, must be EXTREMELY aware of your horse's attention span when teaching this trick. If you notice that your horse is starting to get bored with learning this, then end the trick on a successful "Take It!" and move on to something else. Some horses will never be really good at this because they don't like it. If your horse is one who chooses not to participate, and you really want to pursue fetching then expect to work on this for quite some time.

What to pick up? Horses are not like dogs in that they won't pick up every slimy, hairy thing within reach. They are very particular about what they put in their mouths so you must take this into consideration. I have had good luck using clean, round, plastic, body brushes – the horses seem to like the soft prickles and they like to chew on them once they have them in their mouth. Some other popular "Take It!" items are: cowboy hats, horse balls, squeaky dog toys…you name it. Every horse is different, so, once you have found your item, here is how you teach 'take it'.

Reamo's favorite is his rum bottle, from which he drinks flat cola.

Teaching this trick is all about rewarding 'try'. Stand in front of your horse, hold the object in front of his mouth (touching his lips) and tell him to "Take it". If your horse even twitches his lip then remove the object and give him his treat reward. Again, hold the object in front of his lips, and again ask him to "take it". Once again, reward any movement of your horse's lips.

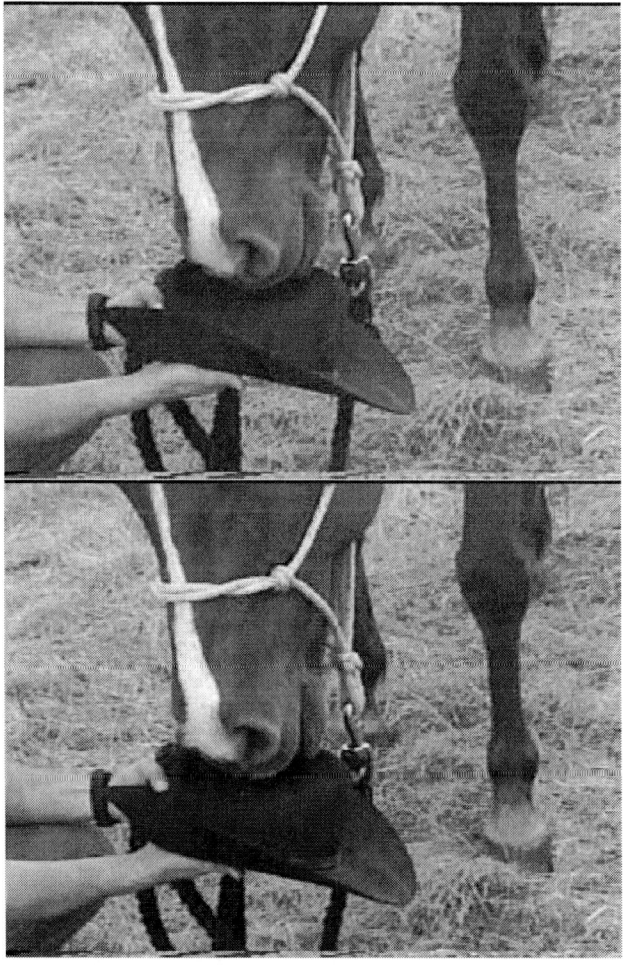

Spot the difference - you'll find only one. The photos are similar, but they tell the story of 100% 'try' - the subtle change of Sally's lips MUST be rewarded otherwise she will quit putting effort into learning this trick. When horse people refer to 'feel', it is the difference between these two photos that they are talking about.

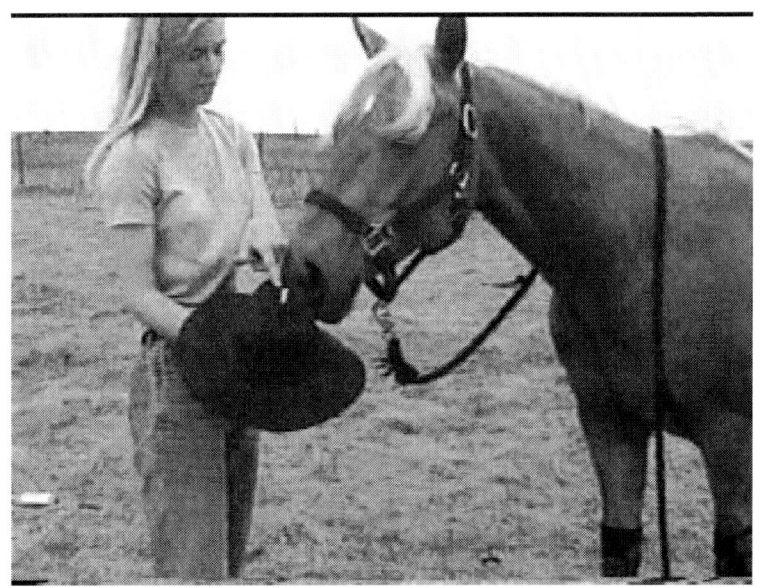

As an added 'bonus' I have put a cookie in the fold of this old coyboy hat. This will encourage Reamo to use his lips and mouth to search for his treat.

I

hold the hat for Reamo and tell him to "take It"

Reamo opens his mouth and takes the hat.

While still maintaining a light hold on the hat, I tell Reamo to "HOLD". Before he lets go, I will tell him to "Release". Over time, I will build up the amount of time that he holds the object. If he drops it without waiting for my 'Release' cue, then I will scold him with a firm 'NO" and ask him to take the hat again.

The most common mistake in training the "take it" is that people try to shove the object into the horse's mouth. You must refrain from doing this, as your horse will simply start to resist your training attempts.

When your horse realizes that he is getting praise for attempting to take the object, he will start to put more effort into taking it. Soon, he will open his mouth and take the object in his teeth to get a taste of what you are offering. When he takes the object in his teeth, immediately ask him to "Release", take the object from his mouth and give him huge praise and reward. The "Take it" can't be taught all in one session. Once you can get your horse to take an object in his teeth (even briefly) end the session and move on to something else.

When you return to training the "take it" again, ask your horse to take the object, then build on having more time between the "take it" and the "release". Reinforce that you want him to keep the object in his mouth by telling him "Hold" ("Hold" is a very important word that is going to be getting a LOT of use later on). Now work on teaching your horse to hold the object for a short length of time.

Once you have extended the time between "take it" and "release," get your horse to start moving out for the object. Start by holding the object a few inches from his mouth so that he has to reach for it rather than you handing it to him. Move the object a little further away and have your horse reach for it. Hold the object down low until you are holding it just off the ground. Remember that each time he takes the object, ask him to release it and then give him his treat reward in exchange for the object in his mouth. If your horse drops the object before you ask for the "release," tell him "No!" then put the object to his lips for him to take it again. Remember DON'T force the object back into his mouth. It will just build resistance.

Once the object is back in his mouth, immediately ask him to release it, then give him his treat reward. You want your horse to learn to associate the word "release" with the treat. Having your horse reach out for an object is sufficient for one training session. Once he reaches out and takes the object a few times, end the session and move on to something else. By now your horse is reaching out and taking objects, which he then holds until you request that he release them. The final step in the "Take it" is to get him to retrieve the object for you. Now that your horse is reaching down, put the object on the ground and have him pick it up from the ground. When he becomes consistent in the ground pick up, move the object, or give it a light toss away from yourself. Point to the object and ask your horse to "take it". Your horse will take a couple of steps, pick up the object, then return to you for his treat.

Notes: When teaching your horse to pick something up, don't be in a rush, and don't try to push your horse beyond his limits. I messed up teaching the "Take it" when I pushed my horse too fast, then got impatient and tried to force the object into his mouth when he dropped it. The only thing I accomplished was putting my horse back to square one with this trick. The "trick" to teaching this trick is to keep it light and fun, and keep the training session short over many days. If you keep your training lighthearted, your horse will start to think that picking things up is his idea and will start to pick things up just to show you how smart he is.

HIDE YOUR HEAD

Requirements: Treat Reward.

Standing in front of your horse, put your right hand on your hip.
Your horse will hide his head under your arm.

As in teaching the 'Hug,' teaching this trick requires a bit of
flexibility on your part. Standing in front of your horse, put
your right hand on your hip and pretend to scold your horse. At
the same time that you are doing this, wrap your left arm around
your back (your left hand should be holding a treat reward).
Your horse should be able to see the treat through the hole that
you have made with your right arm. When he sees the treat he
will put his head under your arm. Give him his treat and tell
him he is wonderful. Practice this until he puts his head under
your arm without hesitation.

As he gets a better understanding of what you want, rely less on
holding the treat behind your back. Pretend to scold him and

put your hand on your hip. Give him a second and if he doesn't put his head under your arm, then cue him with the treat behind your back. Soon, he will know that he gets his treat when he puts his head under your arm.

Traditionally, this trick is presented in conjunction with your horse acting ashamed. However, you can change the mood of this trick. Instead of scolding, ask your horse if he wants to play hide and seek while putting your hand on your hip. Your horse will then "hide" under your arm. Alternatively, you can tell your horse a scary story. Put your hand on your hip and ask what he thinks of your story and he can respond by hiding his head. The possibilities are endless. All you have to do is practice.

Hold bait behind your back and through your arm to entice your horse to hide his head.

After a long day, your horse can shove you home if you don't feel like riding.

SHOVE

Requirements: Treat reward, halter, 2 lead shanks.
Watch Out For: Uninvited pushing and invasion of space.

Stand in front of your horse with your back to him. Lean forward slightly and tell your horse to "push". Your horse will lower his head and shove you forward.

Clip a lead rope in each of the side rings of your horse's halter (this is to guide you, not your horse). Standing in front of your horse, turn your back on him, and with a rope in either hand, back up until your back is resting against his face. Tell your horse to "Push" and when he pushes even a little bit, reach behind you and hand him a treat (don't turn to face him yet). Lean back against him again and request that he push you.

With practice, your horse will place his head well under you to launch you into the air. To encourage the lofty shoves, verbally encourage your horse for the little pushes, and give treat rewards for the airborne ones. The pushing stops when I turn to face Reamo. Uninvited shoving receives a firm NO!

Once again, you have to reward the smallest of tries. Practice this and your horse will get quite a kick out of pushing you. As he becomes more aggressive in his shoving, stop stepping back to lean on his face, and instead encourage him to come to you and give you another shove. When your horse knows to start walking toward you, take the lead shanks off his halter. Remember for every push – light or heavy – give your horse a treat and tell him he's good. Over time, the shove will become more animated and he will follow you around, shoving as he goes. Start to wean him off the treat rewards by having him shove you 2 or 3 times before you turn around and give him his treat. Then, push 4 or 5 times and so on. Eventually, he will push you until you turn and tell him to stop.

As your horse gets more confident in this trick, he will be able to put his head low enough to pick you right off the ground and throw you out of his way. To get animation and height out of the pushes, lean forward so that the only thing to push is your butt. Ask him to push, and if he nudges you with his nose tell him he is a good boy but withhold the treat.

Only give treat rewards for solid, forehead, bunts and your horse will learn to be more aggressive with this trick. When starting this part though, remember to reward 'try,' otherwise a frustrated and confused horse might give a nip over a nudge.

Although it is quite fun to be launched in the air, this trick becomes hard on your back if your horse gives you an unexpected trip into the dirt. Your cue is standing with your back to your horse's face. When you start to train this trick, you will have to be more aware of how you lead your horse. If you are used to towing him along while he plods behind you, you might get a surprising "shot in the shorts". When you start teaching this trick, you should (if you don't already), start leading your horse with his head beside you, rather than dragging along behind. Of equal importance, when you turn to face your horse, the trick is over! Initially, your horse will think that he is supposed to shove you all the time. You must be firm and discipline him if he tries to push you while you are facing him otherwise this trick will become rude and annoying, and the potential is there for someone to get hurt.

Training your horse to drink from a bottle is just a combination of "Take It" and "Yes". The shadow shows that I am standing in front of Reamo cueing him for the "Yes". Generally I will have flat cola in the bottle as an instant 'treat' for Reamo when he 'drinks'. As luck would have it, the day that we took this photo, I had lost his regular rum bottle, and didn't have cola on hand. Improvising is one of the key elements of trick training!

COMBINE YOUR TRICKS

Once you and your horse master a few of these tricks, you can start to put them together in an act. Teaching a horse to drink from a bottle, for example, is just the combination of "take it," and "yes." Ask him to take the bottle from your hand, then give him the "yes" cue and your horse will be drinking from a bottle. If you want to add the reality of liquid and give your horse a treat reward at the same time, use flat pop (cola works well because I always seem to have some old stuff sitting in my fridge). When you first introduce your horse to pop in a bottle, expect him to be surprised and drop the bottle. If your horse isn't really one for surprises, introduce him to the pop by mixing a small amount in with his grain or pouring some in the bottom of his bucket. You don't have to overdo the taste test, just let him try a bit and he'll be hooked…after all, how long did it take you to really get a taste for pop?

If you decide to teach your horse to drink from a bottle, use plastic bottles only. I prefer the slim plastic rum bottles. They don't weigh a lot full, and their design makes it easy to slip them into your back pocket (no kidding!) and out of the way. Also, the plastic molds to your horse's teeth allowing him to lock onto the bottle and hold it easier. I have had folks give me some pretty dirty looks after feeding my horse what appears to be straight rum. I think they believe that I am a hard core alcoholic who's dragging my horse down with me!

Now that you get the idea, trick combinations can be limitless!

LEAD BY THE TAIL

Requirements: Halter, Longe line.
Watch Out For: You are going to be standing directly behind your horse so if you have ANY reservations about him kicking you, don't do this.

Stand behind your horse. Pull his tail toward you and ask him to back. Your horse will back up.

Ok, so it's not really a trick but it surely is handy for him to learn. If you teach your horse to lead by his tail, you can back him out of the horse trailer, out of the standing–stall, and out of strange situations that he has gotten himself into, where you can't get to his head.

You can either teach this in a standing stall or in the open. Attach the longe line to your horse's halter so that you have one long, continuous rein. Standing behind your horse, pull his tail toward you and ask him to back. At the same time that you are pulling his tail, pull back on the longe 'rein'. Initially, your horse will back up from the pressure on his halter. Start to transfer the back up cue to his tail by applying less and less pressure to his halter. Soon, your horse will know to back up with the tail command only. If you have access to a standing stall, teaching this will be extremely easy as the horse will understand that he backs out of the stall – the action will have purpose. Outside a standing-stall will work well also, but expect to spend a little more time.

There is no reason to give a treat reward for your horse leading by his tail. This should be an everyday courtesy like picking up his feet, and standing tied.

Although difficult to depict direction, Reamo complies with my request to back up on a cold winter day.

SECTION II

TRICKS USING THE FRONT LEGS

Well, you are going to figure it out pretty soon that tricks using the front legs are all pretty much the same trick…

A promotional photo of Bonnington Farms Poco Pico sitting down (which is very different from the sit up). Instructions for the sit up are detailed in Section III

MARCH A.K.A. SPANISH WALK

Requirements: Halter, lead rope, bridle, short whip, treat reward.
Watch Out For: Front feet striking out and back.

While riding your horse, jiggle your right rein and ask your horse to "March". Your horse extends his right front leg in an animated, striking walk. Click once with your tongue and repeat the cue with the left rein to get a right-foot, left-foot, high-stepping march.

Teaching your horse to march involves 4 different steps. Firstly, you will start training the march from the ground. Secondly, you will move your command to your horse's bridle reins. Thirdly, you will cue your horse from his back and lastly, you will add forward movement. Don't expect to train your horse to march in one session. The building of the four steps to the conclusion of the final march takes time.

1. TRAINING MARCH FROM THE GROUND

Start training the march from the ground. Standing at your horses left shoulder, take your short whip, and, with the handle end, tap his left cannon bone while asking him to "March!" Your horse will lift his leg in response to you tapping his cannon bone. When he does this, give him a treat reward, offer lots of praise, and stroke the leg that he picked up, to let your horse know that the lifted leg is the response that you are looking for. Repeat this until your horse extends his left leg and starts to paw the ground. Generally, horses that are younger or more dominant will start to paw after only a few taps to their cannon bone. Horses who are more passive or who are older will generally just lift their foot up as if you were asking to pick out their hooves. With horses such as these, start to withhold the treat reward and continue to request the 'March' while tapping the cannon bone until the horse makes a forward movement with his leg. When the horse makes a forward movement, tell him he is good and give him his treat reward.

When you have your horse really striking out and pawing at the ground with just a tap reminder on the left side, then it is time to start from scratch on the right side. Move to the right shoulder and start the 'March' training again. Initially, don't be concerned about how many times your horse paws the ground, the goal is to have him paw, and the amount of times that he strikes out will decrease to one strike. Also worth noting, the cue for your horse to strike out his front foot is not you standing at the respective shoulder. Rather, it is the verbal "March" command with the whip/tap backup that is the cue. If he starts to strike out simply because you have moved to his shoulder, then don't issue the 'March' command. Instead, stand quietly at your horse's shoulder for about 10 – 15 seconds until he settles. Uninvited strikes should be greeted with a firm "STOP!" from you and, if necessary, a disciplinary tap from the whip – the disciplinary tap should be a more firm strike than the tap that you used to request the "March." 'Stop' means 'stop' and the

While temperatures plumet to minus 35, a bundled up Brenda asks Sally to strike out by tapping her cannon bone with a whip. These photos show accelerated training of the March or Spanish Walk.

Once Sally understands the cue from the whip, Brenda asks her to respond to a cue from the bridle only. Due to temperatures, Sally is working in a halter.

whip in this instance is used to remind the horse that you aren't kidding. Once he has stopped striking out uninvited, stand quietly for about10 seconds and then resume schooling.

2. MOVING YOUR CUE TO THE BRIDLE

Once your horse is able to paw/march with both the right and left legs, then it's time to move the cue from his cannon bone to his bridle reins. Put his bridle on, and stand at his left shoulder. Take the left rein in one hand and hold the whip in the other. While telling your horse to "March" jiggle the left rein. Obviously, he won't know what you are requesting so tap his cannon bone with the whip to initiate the "March" response. When he starts to paw/march, give him praise and his treat. Transferring cues from one place to another is just a matter of weaning him off one cue and onto another …in this case, the bridle. Jiggle the rein again and ask for the "March." If he doesn't offer the paw on his own, just explain to him what you are looking for by cueing with the whip. Soon, your horse will paw/march the ground with his left leg when you jiggle the left rein. When he has mastered the rein cue from the left side, then move over to his right shoulder and start again.

When your horse can paw/march using only a rein cue from both the left and right side then it's time to prepare him for the riding cue. Stand at his left shoulder. Request the "March" with the left rein. When he paws/marches, tell him he is a good boy, but withhold the treat reward. Now, stay at his left shoulder and jiggle the right rein. Your horse may paw with his left foot. If this is the case, tell him "Other Foot" and reach over with the whip to tap his right foot. When he paws with his right foot off the right rein cue, tell him how fantastic he is and give him his treat reward. When you start cueing from a single location (on the ground at his left shoulder), your horse will get mixed up with which leg he is supposed to paw with. Have patience, it's kind of like teaching a little kid the difference between his left hand and his right hand. Practice will help your horse learn the difference between right and left.

3. THE RIDING CUE

When you can stand at his left shoulder and cue both the right and left foot using only the respective rein, then it is time to start the riding march. You will still need your whip, so put it in your back pocket or somewhere else where it won't get in the way. At this point, you may have noticed that your horse has a 'favorite foot'. The favorite foot is the foot that he prefers to offer when you cue the "March." When starting the march from his back, cue the favorite foot first. This will set him up to succeed and reduce the chance that he mixes up right and left. For ease or writing, let's just presume that the favorite foot is his left foot.

While sitting on his back, jiggle the left rein and ask him to "March." Obviously, you are asking him to strike out with his left foot, but if he isn't too sure, reach down and tap his cannon bone with the whip to remind him that, even though you are someplace different, the idea is still the same. When he paws with his left foot, tell him he is a good boy and give him his treat reward. Sit up, and jiggle the right rein. Once again, if he doesn't offer his right foot, then lean over and tap his cannon bone with the whip as a reminder. Repeat the cues back and forth until he can give you a stationary march without the additional help of the whip cue.

By now you might be noticing that he has decreased the number of times that he paws the ground. This is normal and soon he will discover that he only needs to strike once to earn his praise and reward.

You can just see the poof of the whip over Sally's extended leg. Brenda cues from the bridle and uses the whip as a back up cue on the mare's cannon bone.

The whip abandoned (bottom right corner) Brenda uses exaggerated bridle cues to achieve the strike. With practice, the bridle cue will be invisible.

4. FORWARD MOVEMENT

Now that your horse is marching in place, it's time to add forward movement. You might have discovered that when your horse is doing his stationary march, his front legs are getting farther and farther away from his back legs. All you have to do to achieve forward movement is get his back legs to keep up with his front legs! Ask your horse for his left leg march. Once he delivers it, click with the back of your tongue and apply leg pressure to get your horse to step forward with his back legs. Then, ask for the right leg march, click and apply leg pressure. If your horse isn't down to one striking paw by now, he will soon be when he associates the click with your satisfaction that one strike is good enough. If, however, your horse tries to test the waters on delivering a lackluster, lazy strike, then remind him that you need a little more effort. Go back to your backup cue and tap the offending leg with the whip or the end of your reins (if they are long enough). After taking a couple of steps, reward your horse and tell him he is good. Build up the amount of marching steps slowly over time until you can travel a straight line down the length of an arena. Adding forward movement is a coordinated effort for your horse, so it's going to be a little choppy for the first while. Have patience, practice lots and don't worry if your marching horse takes you in a strange zig-zaggy pattern. Soon you will have a very pretty march.

Compare 'Cash' above with 'Reamo' centre. In the same striking step, Cash is somewhat strung-out in the back while Reamo (middle) engages his hind foot to accommodate the movement of his front leg. Keeping the hind end working with the front end allows for a more fluid march. In this photo of Cash, the march step is choppy while he learns to work his front and back legs together. Depending upon the build of your horse, your march will be more animated or more mello. Quarter Horses, with their heavy build tend to have a less elaborate march. Compare the strike of the QH's to 'Spike' the Welsh pony (bottom). Although his short black leg doesn't stand out, the extension of his leg is much more animated thanks to his naturally high headset.

Once again, we see the progression of forward movement. At the start of the march, when the leg is most curled, Cash (top) is somewhat strung out behind, while Reamo (middle) works his hind end with his front end. Once again, we compare to our Welsh pony Spike (bottom) to appreciate the elevation that comes with different body builds. High head set equals high hoof strike.

61

The march is a very handy trick to teach a horse. If my horse doesn't give me his attention, I request the march to regain control and get him to focus on the task at hand. If it's the first ride of the season and he is feeling a little springy, I request the march to allow him to blow off some steam while still maintaining control. If a horse wants to rush home during a trail ride, requesting the march will force him to burn off the excess energy for a more enjoyable ride. Basically, the march is a very versatile tool. Traditionally, riders were taught to back their horse up to get control, restore focus or slow an exuberant horse. I prefer the march over the back up because it keeps the rider moving forward rather than backing up into ditches, fences, walls or who knows what. Also, backing an excited horse puts them in the proper position for a rear whereas the horse would never entertain the thought of rearing during a march.

On a cold, cold day, I use the March to keep Reamo's attention on me while riding bareback and bridle-less

COUNT

Requirements: Halter, lead rope, bridle, short whip, treats
Watch Out For: Front feet striking out.

 From the ground, or while riding, ask your horse how old he is. Jiggle the left rein and your horse will paw (count) the answer.

Once you have taught your horse how to march, counting is the same cue. The only difference between counting and marching is how long you jiggle the rein cue. When counting, you are only working with one leg, don't click to get the forward movement, just drop the rein to stop the action.

You can make your cue different from that of the march cue, or make it very subtle, by transferring the cue to that of your liking by following the same steps in the march sequence where you transferred the cue from the cannon bone to the bridle. Don't forget the backup cue on the cannon bone is still there and will be there for the rest of his life. If you want to start from scratch with your count cue, then use the cue on his cannon bone as a starting place from which to transfer to the new cue. After you have done the transfer, and established the new cue, practice will make perfect. Your horse will stop counting when you stop cueing.

*Nature's Pedestal -
Standing on a flat
rock in the North
Saskatchewan River*

PEDESTAL WORK

Requirements: Halter, longe line, long whip, treat reward, pedestal.

Watch Out For: Horse striking, jumping over pedestal, jumping onto pedestal, horse crowding you to avoid getting on pedestal.

While near a pedestal, tell your horse "Go Step". Your horse will walk to the pedestal and step up with his front feet. Tell your horse to "Step Up" and he will put his back feet on the pedestal as well, if size permits.

First you have to determine what you would like to use for a pedestal. A safe pedestal is large enough that your horse can step on it without his feet being crowded. It is sturdy enough that it won't tip should your horse step on the edge of it. It is strong enough to support the entire weight of your horse, as well as resilient enough to handle him pawing at it with his front feet. A safe pedestal is also light enough that YOU can easily move it. When working with pedestals, I use a large bridge that was built for trail class, or smaller, round pedestals.. Whatever you decide to use for your pedestal, just ensure that it is stable, strong, and that the surface is not slippery.

Angle Iron Clips 1"

3/4" Plywood

Old Tire Rim. Flip upside down so that the weight is at the bottom, then fasten wood

Don't spend a lot of money on constructing your pedestal. You should be able to make one for under $20. The items that you need to gather are:

- **1 Old Tire Rim (15" or so).** Make sure that the rim is metal not aluminum and not fancy. You need it to sit flat on both sides - and you have to weld on it.
- **2 – 1" Pieces of 1" Angle Iron.**
- **¾" Plywood**. Depending upon the size of your tire rim, you will only need enough to cut a 15" inch circle. Measure the inside diameter of your tire rim to determine the exact size. You want the plywood to sit inside of the lip of the rim (see diagram) and rims are measured in 14, 15 or 16" as a general rule.

You will also need a ruler, a sharpened pencil, an awl or sharp nail, a piece of string (about 10 - 12" long), a jig saw and someone who knows how to weld.

Flip your tire rim so that the shallow end is on the floor and the deep end is upright (completely opposite to the tire rim in the diagram). Measure the diameter of the rim, resting your ruler on the lip/ledge, just inside the outermost diameter. Tie the string to the awl and the pencil so that the tips, when you pull the string tight, measure ½ the total diameter or radius of the tire rim. Put one pencil in the center of your plywood piece, and run the pencil around in a circle, keeping your string tight. Ta Da! You now have a circle that should measure the same diameter as your tire rim.

Use your jig saw to carefully cut along the pencil line. When you have your plywood circle cut out, try it for size. Place it in the tire rim (per the diagram) so that it sits firmly on the lip/ledge inside outermost dimension. Finally, get your welder buddy to weld the 2 clips onto the rim, pinching the plywood in place. The heat from the weld will 'shrink' the clips so that they are snug on the wood, holding it securely. If you find that your wood starts to loosen, take a good sized hammer and give your clips a wack to tighten them back up again. When welding, have a spray bottle of water handy just in case the heat from the welding starts your wood on fire.

If you absolutely do not know anyone who welds and have no clue what a jig saw is, take heart! There are a lot of potential pedestals in the world. Find a good sized flat rock (one that you can lift, or one that is never going to move but is close enough to work on). Anything can be a pedestal as long as it can safely hold the weight of your horse.

If you are always going to work in the same place, an old tire, filled, and packed with sand, or dirt, will also work as a stationary pedestal.

When introducing your horse to the pedestal, you want him to learn that the pedestal is a place of rest and good eats. Place a small amount of grain in the center of the pedestal and have your horse walk up to it. If your horse is really concerned about that thing sitting on the ground, then just be calm, and encourage him to approach it. Once your horse gets close enough, he will discover that there is a treat waiting for him on that scary thing and all of a sudden the pedestal will become a friendlier place in your horse's mind. When he has accepted that the pedestal won't eat him, stand him in front of it and encourage him to "Step". Step up on the pedestal yourself, feed your horse treats, and tell him how good he is. Ask your horse to "Step". He probably won't, but he is going to get used to hearing that word. Get off the pedestal and ask your horse to "Step". Take his front foot and place it on the pedestal. As soon as you place his hoof on the pedestal, stroke his leg and say "Hold." Don't forget to tell him he is a good boy. Feed him a treat to reinforce the fact that the closer he is to this thing, the more he gets fed. Continue to place his foot for him until he stops removing it. Reinforce that you don't want that foot to move by telling him to "Hold". Once he starts to relax, tell him "Good Boy!" If he removes his foot from the pedestal, tell him "No" and withhold the treat reward until he "Holds!" Put his foot back up and tell him to "hold". When he consistently keeps his foot on the pedestal, walk in front of him and gently tug on his halter and lead shank to get him to straighten his lifted leg which will cause him to step up. Of course, when he shifts his weight and steps up, tell him he is the greatest and give him lots of treat rewards. Let him stand with his two front feet on the pedestal. Brush him and feed him and just generally let him relax for as long as he wants. The idea is for your horse to learn that the pedestal is the most relaxing place in the world. After a bit, ask your horse to step off the pedestal. Take him for a short walk around, and, when you return to the pedestal, ask him to "Step". You might have to place and 'hold' his foot a few more times, but soon your horse will learn to step onto the pedestal himself. If your horse is telling you that he wants to get on the pedestal but just isn't too sure of what to do, don't forget about all that you learned when you taught him the march. With your whip, tap the cannon bone, which will cause your horse to strike up and out…and, if you have lined up properly, he will smack his foot down right on top of the pedestal. Even if he doesn't keep his foot on the pedestal, he did take the initiative to try getting up without your help so reward him as if he were standing on top of it.

Once your horse puts his own foot on the pedestal, you can't backtrack and put his foot up for him. The only time this is allowed is if you are changing your pedestal to something drastically different. If you resort back to placing his foot, your horse will soon learn that you are a pushover and he will always rely on you to do the work for him. Ask your horse again to "Step". If necessary, tap his cannon bone with the whip. After a few tries, ask him for more effort. Instead of rewarding him with the treat, just tell him he is a good boy – you always want him thinking about what he can do to get that food reward. Stand in front of him with the pedestal between you and ask him to "step". When he steps with the one foot, tug on his halter and get him to step up with the other foot. Now, you can feed him and offer great amounts of praise. Practice will have your horse stepping up with great confidence. Don't forget to practice from all sides of the pedestal. When starting, most horses think that the side that they first stepped up on is the only side that they can get up on, so don't be surprised when your horse gets a little balky going a different direction.

If your horse just doesn't want to take the responsibility of getting onto the pedestal himself, then you can reinforce that: off the pedestal is work, on the pedestal is rest and food. Attach your longe line to your horses halter and ask him to longe. He should be longing at a brisk trot – this isn't a leisurely thing, he should be working. Tell your horse to stop in front of the pedestal walk up to him and tell him to "Step".

Accelerated pedestal training. I get young 'Duster' (8 months old) used to holding his foot on the pedestal. After placing his foot on the ped, I pet his 'good' leg and tell him to hold. If your horse starts to repeatedly jerk his foot from your hand, don't be afraid to tell him NO in a firm voice and swat his 'bad' leg with the tips of your fingers. On the other hand, don't discourage a horse who likes to pound the ped with his front foot, you will need this enthusiasm when it comes time for him to mount the ped without your help.

When Duster shows me that he is comfortable holding his foot on the ped, I ask him to step forward by applying pressure to his lead shank. When applying pressure, don't be tentative about it, simply act as if you are walking forward.

With pressure on his lead shank, I am constantly telling Duster to "STEP". Sometimes the horse will just leave his leg dangling in the air, not sure where to place it. When this happens, quickly place his leg on the pedestal for him.

Success! Duster is on the pedestal. I will now let him relax up there by feeding him treats and releasing all pressure on his lead shank. You can even let the lead shank drop to the ground.

The road to climbing aboard a pedestal isn't always smooth. Young Duster has to learn where to place his feet, and as we see in this sequence of photos, he hasn't quite figgured it out yet. Stepping on the edge, he slips off the ped and gets tangled in it. There is no need to panic, just let him get himself untangled and continue on.

The second most common occurrence is missing the ped all together. In this sequence, Duster can't see where to place his feet and tries to compensate by jumping over the ped. You can minimize occurrences of this by starting a few feet back and walking your horse up to the ped so that he can see it clearly.

After lining up again, Duster makes his last attempt on the pedestal.....

72

.....and succeeds! Finishing off with a nice, flamboyant salute from a verbal cue. Once a horse figures out how to get up on his own, it's not something that he generally forgets.

Use the whip to touch his cannon bone and get the high stepping strike. If he strikes the pedestal, he gets a treat and praise. If he would rather dance around and avoid it, get him moving on the longe line again. This is where you really have to understand your horse. The only reason that you should employ the use of the longe line is if your horse is being lazy. If your horse is honestly afraid of the pedestal, then running him around in circles isn't going to help the situation. Resort to the longe line if your horse has been stepping on the pedestal, but then decides not to participate, or just kind of lazily steps all around it. The longe line is just to remind your horse that the alternative to getting on the pedestal takes a lot more effort.

If your pedestal is large enough to comfortably accommodate all four feet, and strong enough to support the entire weight of your horse, then you can get him to stand on all four. Start by having your horse walk over the pedestal after he has been standing on it with his front feet. Basically, treat your pedestal as a bridge. When you are walking over the pedestal, tell your horse to "Step Up", he will start to associate the verbal command with moving his back legs forward and up. Use the halter to stop the forward motion of your horse as he is coming over the pedestal and reward him with treats and praise when he has either three or all four feet on the pedestal.

When you have your horse stepping on the pedestal from the ground, have him step onto it while you are riding him. Once your horse knows that the pedestal is a pretty neat place to be, he will be happy to step onto it with little assistance from you. Once again, it just comes down to practice!

Spike and TJ both step up onto the bridge ped.

74

Completely at liberty, Spike, the 1.5 year old Welsh cross, steps up and onto the pedestal.

This is the finished product. Notice that Spike isn't working in a pen or an arena. he is working in 80 acres. His performance on the pedestal is truely at liberty.

Now that your horse is mounting the pedestal, let's learn how to teach the snappy salute.

Reamo (foreground) offers a tucked salute at liberty while Sally (background) offers her salute in hand. Off camera, Brenda is transferring Sally's cue from her halter to the air. The whip is there for backup to reinforce the salute.

SALUTE

Requirements: Long whip, treat reward.
Watch Out For: Front feet striking out

While your horse is standing on his pedestal, hold the butt end of your whip up and ask him to salute. Your horse will raise his front leg in a curled salutation.

Stand in front of your horse (back about 3 or 4 feet so that he doesn't accidentally hit you with his foot) while he is standing with his front legs on his pedestal. Ask your horse to salute and tap the cannon bone of his right leg. From the training of the "March," your horse will know that a touch on the cannon bone means that he raises that leg. Initially, he will try to strike with his front foot, but finding no ground to paw into, will leave his leg dangling in the air. Give him his praise and reward for a job well done. Your horse will immediately understand what you want of him, and the only thing that is left is to shape the behavior to make it prettier. Hold the butt end of your whip at shoulder level and ask your horse to "Salute." If he doesn't, flick the whip toward his cannon bone. Practice and soon your horse will curl his front leg when he sees the butt end of the whip being held up.

After you have been practicing for a while, work on getting greater lift from your horse's leg. Tell your horse "Bigger!" and reward him when he holds his leg higher, steadier, or longer. If he just kind of hangs his leg in the air, flick the cannon bone to emphasize your desire for more animation in the salute. You can also cue your horse to salute while you are riding him. Ride your horse onto the pedestal and jiggle the right rein while telling him to "Salute". Instead of continuing to jiggle the rein, hold it up with some tension and your horse will respond by holding his leg up in the air. Very shortly your horse will learn to salute when he steps onto the pedestal and the action will become almost automatic.

After mounting his ped at liberty, Spike offers a snappy salute while I cue him off camera.

From left to right: Eyore (9 month old Jack Donkey), Duster (9 month old Quarter Horse stud colt), Bella (9 month old Welsh/Arab filly), Midnight (9 month Welsh filly), and Pico (8 month old Donkey Jenny) - Breeder: Melita Clemence of Bonnington Farms. The group stands on their pedestals, and pose for the camera. It is 32 below zero, and their breath creates a fog that hangs in the air. This group started trick training when they were weanlings. Now, at 9 months they will step onto their pedestals at liberty.

Reamo turns on the front, twising his legs .

TWIST FRONT LEGS

Requirements: Halter, lead rope, treat reward, a horse that knows how to turn on the forehand.
Watch Out For: Horse stumbling and losing balance.

Ask your horse to turn on the forehand. He will execute the turn while keeping his front feet stationary, resulting in his front legs winding up. Your horse will be left standing with his front legs crossed until you unwind him.

Get your horse used to having his legs crossed by picking up his foot and crossing it over his leg. Stroke his leg and tell him to "Hold!". If your horse uncrosses his legs, take it again and tell him to hold while placing it back over top of his stationary leg. When your horse can stand comfortably with his legs crossed, it's time to wind him up.

Stand your horse up so that he is standing square on all four legs. Stroke both of his front legs and tell him to "Hold". Ask him to move his hind end one step to the right, then return to his front legs and tell him he is good for holding them there. Give your horse a treat and praise while you pet his 'good' front legs. Ask him to move his hind end another step to the right. Return to his stationary legs, praise your horse and give him treats. You will probably get about three or four hind end steps to the right before your horse blows it and moves his front foot. If your horse moves his front foot, swat the cannon bone with your hand to let him know that you are displeased. Don't offer praise or treat rewards. Instead, pet his front legs and tell him "Hold", then immediately move him a step or two around his front end. When he holds his legs stationary again, offer praise and treats.

When your horse is able to turn on the front while holding his front legs stationary, at his furthest point he will probably have one leg firmly underneath him and the other stretched out in front of him. This will probably be the point where he chickens out and moves the stretched out leg back underneath him. At this point you have two options. You can keep on the training path that you have been following and just continue to ask for the stationary legs and the turn on the front, or you can help your horse by placing his foot by using a rope.

If you are turning on the front by moving your horse's hip to the right (applying pressure to his left side), then his right leg will be the stationary/support leg, and his left leg will end up crossed over his right leg. The left, twisting leg, is the one to which you want to offer support when it is stuck out in front of your horse with nowhere left to go. When your horse is standing square on all four legs, loop a soft cotton lead rope (or a single hock hobble if you have one) around the ankle of his left, front leg. Run the rope across his chest so that it comes up on the right side of his neck and over his withers. Ask him to turn on the front to the furthest point that he turns before he blows it and have him stand there a second. Take up the slack in the rope (that is running down his right shoulder and across his chest to his left leg), and ask him to turn on the front some more. Instead of letting him move his left leg where he wants, use the rope to guide the left leg into position – crossed over his right, supporting leg. Offer tons of praise and a good treat reward. Practice a couple more times until your horse knows that he is supposed to keep his left front leg relaxed and wind it over his right, supporting leg. When he no longer relies on the rope for guidance and support, remove it and teach your horse to twist in the other direction.

If your horse steps out of the twisty legs, scold him and swat the offending leg with your hand so that he knows you are unimpressed. Do not offer praise or treat. Immediately, twist your horse back up again and insist that he stands there until you go around to the other side and untwist him. Finish the turn on the front so that both feet are flat on the ground. Never let your horse walk out of the twisty legs until his feet are flat on the ground. It just creates a bad habit.

It will take time for your horse to find his balance with this trick. Give him time, have patience, and allow him the freedom necessary to find his balance to accomplish the twisty legs. When your horse is dead solid on winding and unwinding his legs, you can transfer this trick to saddle. Initially, it helps to have an assistant guide your horse on the ground while you sit *quietly* in the saddle. Slowly transfer the cue from the ground to the saddle by incorporating the rein and leg necessary to achieve a turn on the front. Turning on the front and ending up with twisty legs is extremely difficult for a horse being ridden as the rider, wiggling around and delivering the cue, messes up his balance. Horse and rider need to practice a lot to get this trick consistent and polished

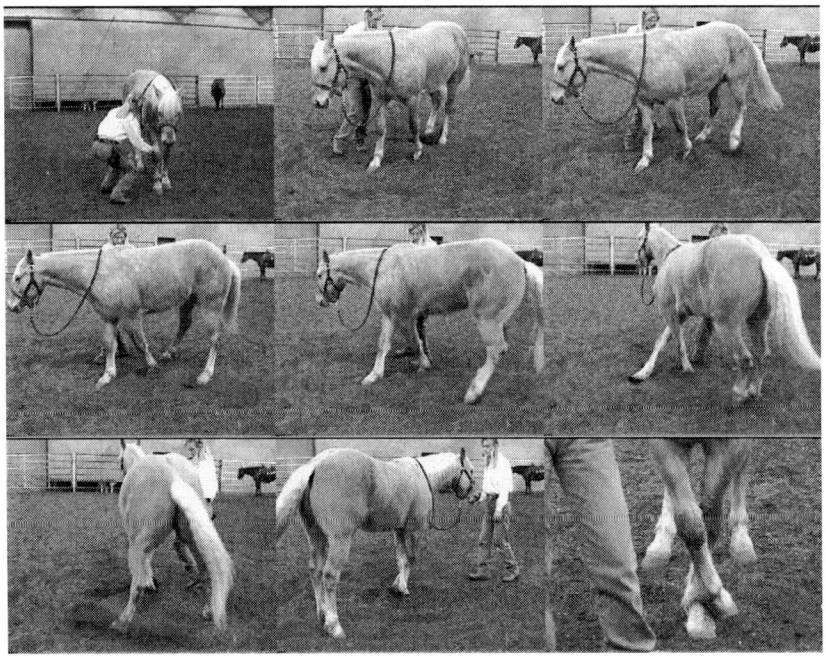

From left to right. After telling Reamo to HOLD, I ask him to turn on the front. As he turns, he keeps his front feet stationary resulting in a corkscrew. The end result is that his legs cross each other.

BODY TRICKS

The "Bow" is the building block of all the Body Tricks. In order for your horse to learn the "Bow" he must pick up each foot individually and hold it until you decide that you are done with it. If your horse can't do this, then he is going to end up jerking you around and you are going to get hurt. Believe me and learn from my experiences, you CAN'T hold up a 1000 pound horse if he decides that he's had enough and starts to flail around. Make it easy on yourself and get him picking up his feet properly. When your horse gives you the "Bow," and then the "Lie-Down," he is showing you the ultimate in trust. After a horse has learned to lie down, he seems to experience a mental maturity. For this reason, the "Bow" should be introduced with calm consideration. Make your horse's first experience with the "Bow" a pleasurable one, not a frightening one. After learning the "Bow" and "Lie-Down," the relationship that you have with your horse will be on a more personal level. Ensure that during this segment of training you do everything possible to protect the trust that you will earn.

A "Bow" goes wrong at a youth clinic and I am pitched forward onto Reamo's neck. Reamo got his legs crossed up on the way down, throwing himself off balance and throwing me off his back. Always expect the unexpected...especially when you THINK that you know what you are doing!

Training a horse to perform 'body stunts' is like training a person to do gymnastics - both require flexibility. Just as an older adult, can't be expected to bend like a 3 year old child, don't expect your older horse (older than 4) to be as flexible as a younger horse. Many people these days incorporate flexion as part of riding training as we teach our horses to give to the bit. Bending the head and neck to the right and left, and rounding their frame in collection all help the horse to be more supple and fluid in his movements. For any horse, (and older horses in particular) we can incorporate this flexion into stunt training. Using treats, bait your horse to encourage him to flex his head and neck to either side of his girth, and to his chest. We have already accomplished this for one side when we trained the hug, now we can take the opportunity to ensure that our horse is flexible all the way around. Have him reach high (something that you will have already started when training the kiss) and low for his treat reward. By training your horse to follow his treat to his girth and chest, you are also preparing him for reaching for bait in conjunction with training for the "Bow" (without the use of mechanical aids).

Another stretching 'exercise' (illustrated below) that your horse will enjoy is stretching his legs. Stretching your horses back legs put you in the perfect position to be kicked, so don't attempt this exercise unless you are 100% confident that your horse has exemplary ground manners.

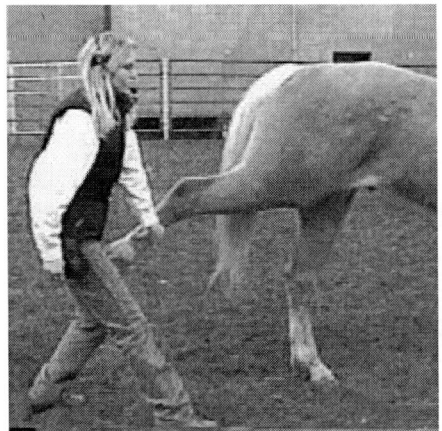 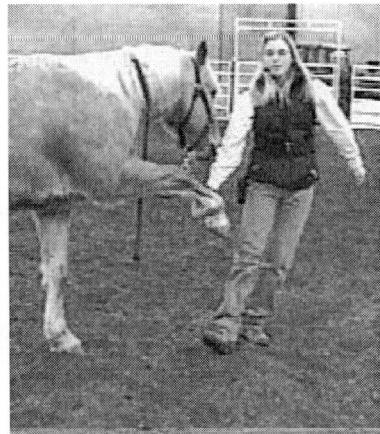

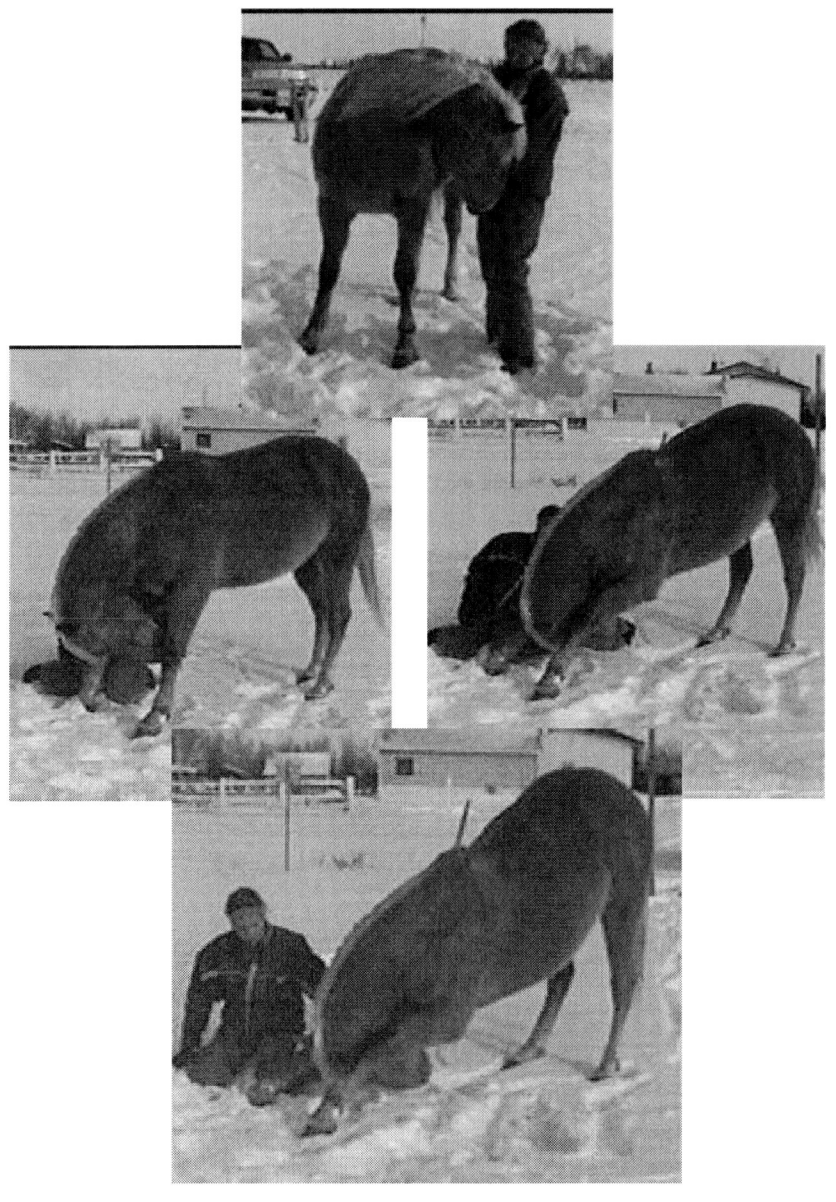

Stretching your horse keeps him flexible. By stretching Reamo to his girth (both sides) and to his chest, he soon becomes flexible enough to reach right between his front legs for his treat.

86

A finished bow needs no equipment and can be cued from a distance.

BOW

Requirements: Soft ground, protective leg/knee wraps
Optional Requirements: Three lead ropes, halter, lots of treat rewards, and hock hobble
Watch Out For: Falling horse, lunging horse, horse off balance

Standing on the right side of your horse, tap his shoulder and tell him "Bow!" Your horse will lift his left front leg and bow.

There are many ways to teach the "Bow." I will explain the three ways that I use most often. First of all, you need to decide if you prefer to use no mechanical aids, a small amount, or a very gentle rig – a running "V". Second, you have to determine if your horse is left or right handed. That said, I have to stop a second and speak on mechanical aids. For seven years I taught horses to Bow while using no mechanical aid whatsoever. Although time consuming, it was an effective way of teaching the trick. At the time, I had no time constraints and spending 30 days on the Bow was acceptable to me. At the end of the 30 days my back was so destroyed that I could barely walk and each Bow session ended with me hobbling away, slowly trying to get back to an upright position. I had it in my mind that using mechanical aids of any sort would be a great disservice to the horse which with I was working, as he was displaying so much trust by giving me the Bow, the least I could do was sweat it out with him. It took me a few years to realize that the only one I was doing a disservice to was myself! I now employ the use of a simple running "V". The running "V" does not trip the horse up. It allows a person to hold the weight of his horse using a pulley idea. I can now teach the Bow in less than 3 days with the help of the running "V". I believe that the running "V" provides more support to the horse when he is first learning the Bow, and it allows the handler to better place the horse's leg when the animal is moving back and down, thus providing the horse with a greater sense of security. I will explain the three methods that I have used. Please read through all of them. There are some problems associated with each method. I have provided some hints that you might find useful should you encounter difficulties while training. My preference is the last method, which uses the help of the running "V".

I teach horses to "Bow" on their right leg for 2 reasons. The first reason is that most horses prefer to lie down on their right sides so teaching the "Bow" on the right hand side sets both you and your horse up for the "Lie-Down." The second reason is that keeping cues on the right hand side ensure that nothing interferes with your riding and handling work, which takes place mostly on the left. So, is your horse 'right handed' or 'left handed'? The way I determine preference is to observe. Pay attention to which side your horse prefers when he is lying down – right or left? If you find that he is usually lying down on his right side then teach him to "Bow" and "Lie-Down" on that side. If your horse prefers to lay on his left side most of the time then you might want to consider his preference and have him "Bow" and "Lie-Down" to his left, so why not use that to your advantage.

Another thing of extreme importance when teaching the "Bow" is, you MUST take precautions to protect the knees and shins of your horse. Most dirt is abrasive and if you don't protect your horse's shins he will get sore very fast and refuse to "Bow" – understandably so! Before you start, get those legs wrapped up.

Lastly, when you are teaching the "Bow" you must tell your farrier of your plan. When a horse starts to understand the "Bow", he will offer it whenever the "trained" leg is lifted. Imagine your farrier's surprise if your horse starts to bow while getting his feet trimmed. To avoid the confusion between the "Bow" and everyday footwork, keep them both separate. "Bow" with the right front foot, and start your hoof cleaning and trimming with the left front foot.

Those are the cautions now, lets move on to the instructions.

1. BOWING WITH NO MECHANICAL AID

You will need a big bucket of treats handy when teaching the "Bow" without mechanical aids. It will save you running back and forth. You will also need to protect the knees and shins of your horse. Use your splint boots. Put the splint boots on upside down (one on each leg) so that the large round part covers your horses knee, and the heavy padding runs down the front of his cannon bone.

Stand at your horse's right shoulder and get him used to reaching back. From the stretching exercises, you learned to use a treat to draw his head back toward his shoulder, and have him bend his neck to take a treat from between his legs. When your horse understand that the treat is waiting just near his shoulder its time to start the "Bow." This is another trick where you have to reward 'try'. Often your horse will offer just a mild lean or shift of weight, but this is actually a milestone and if you don't recognize that, your horse will stop trying and you will not be able to progress into the final bow. So, you must be attentive and reward the slightest shift of weight.

Pick up your horse's right front foot and direct his attention to the fact that there is a treat waiting for him at his shoulder. As he reaches back for the treat, his natural action will be to shift his weight backward, which will result in a lean. When he leans even the slightest let him take the treat, and let him rock back up. Let his foot down gently and tell him he is good! Repeat this a few more times to get your horse used to rocking back on three legs, and get him trusting that nothing bad is going to happen to him.

Now, it's time to incorporate the beginning of the shoulder cue. As you are picking up your horse's foot, tap his shoulder. At this time you will probably realize that it would be easier if you had three arms! When you have his hoof in hand, ask him to lean back to reach the treat. When you find that he is leaning back with more confidence ask him to lean back further and further until his leg is resting on the ground. There is going to be a lot of leaning back and forth when you first start. Your horse won't touch the ground with his foot all in one attempt, but each time he comes back give him his reward and let him rise again. On the next attempt, ask him to rock back just a fraction further before giving him his treat, praise, and allowing him up. Each "Bow" attempt should have your horse moving farther and farther until his leg is able to rest on the ground.

Once his leg is on the ground, immediately tell him to "Hold" and get his mind on staying down by offering him multiple treat rewards. If your horse seems to back track, withhold the treat reward and just give him verbal encouragement until he returns to the farthest point before he rocks back up again. The challenge is to keep pushing your horse past the farthest point that he is willing to rock, then reward him the very millisecond before he decides to chicken out. It's a real balancing act! Once your horse is able to perform a bow, skip forward to Finishing the Bow near the end of this section.

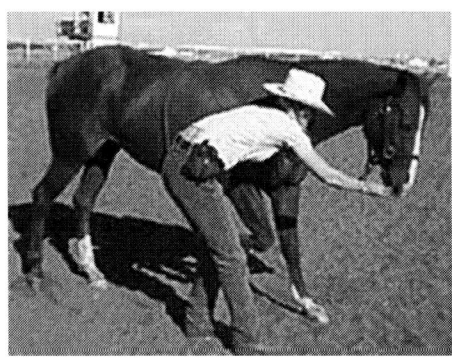

Working in deep, soft ground, I first start the bow with Kassie by picking up her front foot and drawing her head back with treats. Notice how this mare has her hind legs well back to allow her the stance to shift backwards. The lead shank that you see is not being used for the "Bow." It has simply been tossed over her withers and could have actually been removed.

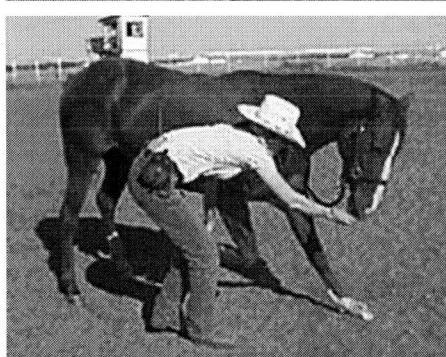

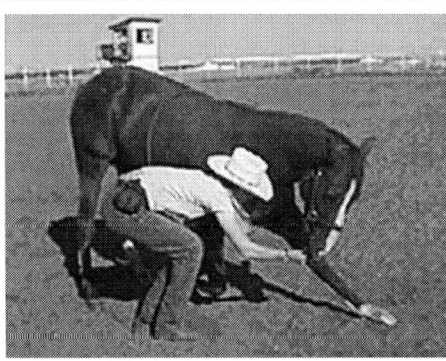

This picture sequence is accelerated. Training a horse to bow without mechanical aids can take as little as a few hours and as long as a few weeks depending upon the level of trust you have in the relationship with your horse.

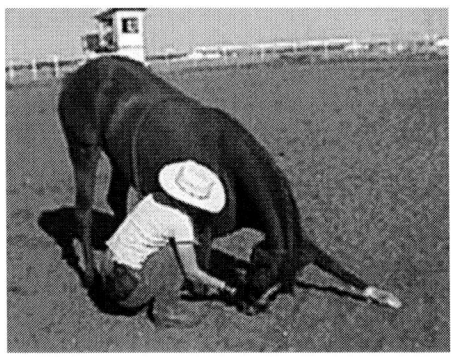

I keep Kassie in the bow by feeding her treats and telling her to Hold!

POTENTIAL PROBLEMS:

My horse was trying but now he ignores the treat - Your horse has lost his attention span. Ask for one more "Bow", and accept whatever he is willing to give (even if it's a pathetic attempt) and then stop training. You have spent a little too much time training the "Bow" and now he is tired and bored. The reason that you ask for just one more "Bow" is so that he understands that you are the one calling the shots and ending the session, not he.

My horse almost touches the ground with his leg but then gets nervous and jumps up - Help him by setting his foot down to let him know that the ground is right there and he isn't going to fall. Once he regains his confidence ask him to lean back further to complete the "Bow".

My horse is trying to bow but his back legs are too close to his front legs and he is running out of room – Help him engage his back end by tapping the cornet band of his back foot with your toe. This will cause him to take a step back allowing him room to lean back.

My horse just jerks his foot out of my hands and walks away – If your horse was previously doing as you asked, but then started to jerk his foot away, ask for one more "Bow." Accept a less than perfect attempt and end training for the day. It could be that your horse is tired and bored. If, however, he always jerks his foot away, then you need to work a little more on having him pick up and hold his foot until you tell him it's time to put it down.

My horse leans back so far but won't lean back any further – Are you rewarding his try? Pay attention to your horse. He might be offering and you just aren't rewarding. You have to learn to read your horse and always push him past the furthest point that he is willing to lean. Try withholding the treat reward and just offer verbal praise so that he learns that he has to work for his food reward.

My horse can reach the treat by curling his body, but he doesn't lean back – Your horse is very supple. You can try holding the treat reward near his chest or between his front legs, or you might want to consider the second described bowing method.

My horse was "Bowing" just fine but then quit for no reason. He has started to really resist my requests to "Bow" – Check his knees for scrapes or other signs of tenderness. If a horse was "Bowing" successfully and then quits suddenly, suspect that he is hurting. If he has a circular patch of wet hair just below his knee, this indicates that he is developing a sore. You will have to re-assess the ground that you are working in and/or modify the leg wraps that you have on your horse so that they offer better protection.

━━━━━━━━━━━━━━━━━

Well, by now you have either a bowing horse or you have a sore back and a horse who just won't get past a certain point. This is understandable, although I can tell you the mechanics of getting your horse to bow, I can't tell you how to read subtle shifts in weight. I also can't explain how you know if your horse has lost his attention span or if he just isn't confident enough to complete the bow. If your horse seems to have reached a plateau in his learning then I'm afraid that you have messed up. You either aren't spending enough time on the "Bow" (it should be worked on every day until it's learned), or you haven't given your horse credit for something that he was offering you during the training and now he has quit. Likewise, maybe you haven't been using enough pressure and your horse has learned that he can get YOU to quit after a certain point and still suck the treat out of you. If this is where you stand, you might want to incorporate the use of simple 'mechanical' aids.

2. BOWING WITH THE HELP OF SIMPLE MECHANICAL AIDS.

As with the previous method, "Bowing" with the help of simple mechanical aids requires that you have soft, deep ground, a bucket of treats, and protective wrapping on your horses legs. This method will also require 2 lead ropes and a halter.

You are going to use the 2 lead ropes to pick up your horses right front foot, and shift the bulk of his weight onto that foot which will help place him into a bow. To get a feeling for what I'm trying to describe, stand up. Lift your right foot off the ground and turn your head to look at your left hip. You will feel your weight moving to your right foot (which should still be off the ground if you haven't fallen over already).

Stand at your horse's withers facing his right shoulder. Your horse should be wearing his halter, and there should be one lead rope running from the halter ring, along the left side of his neck and over his withers. If you pull the rope toward you, your horse should turn his head to the left. The use of the second rope is optional, but recommended. Use the second rope as an extension of your arm to pick up and hold your horses right front foot. Don't tie the rope around his pastern, just wrap the rope around once and hold on to both ends (in the event of a problem, you want the rope around your horse's foot to fall free). The reason that I recommend the use of the rope around his pastern is because you are going to be shifting your horse's weight towards you. You can just hold his leg up with your hand if you so prefer, but if your horse falls down, you will have more time to get out of the way if you are using the second rope to hold his leg.

Take a few minutes to get him used to having his leg picked up with the rope. Tap his shoulder and tell him "Foot" then lift his foot off the ground. Soon, your horse will learn to lift his foot up when you tap on his shoulder – this is preliminary to getting him to "Bow" using just a shoulder cue. Once he is used to having his leg held with a rope, ask him to "Bow" and you tip his nose toward the left by gently pulling on the lead that is running to his halter. Your horse will have no choice but to shift his weight over and back. When your horse leans even the slightest amount, release all the ropes and praise him with your voice and his treats. When using the ropes to shift his weight, you must have patience and not rush him into the "Bow" too fast. Progress so you do not make your horse feel threatened as he will feel that you are pulling him off balance.

A soft, cotton rope is looped around Kassies' ankle. Another lead rope runs from her halter, over her withers. Before starting the "Bow," it is important to have a healthy, trusting relationship with your horse. If you discover that training the "Bow" is nothing but an all out battle it could be time to consider who really has the upper hand, you or your horse.

Not putting any pressure on the rope running to her halter, I get Kassie used to having her foot picked up and held with the soft cotton rope around her ankle. All the while I am picking up her foot, I am asking her to "Bow." You can see from Kassie's ear set that she is listening to me.

Once Kassie is used to having her foot handled with the rope, I apply pressure to the halter rope, which shifts her weight and causes her to lean

backward. Depending upon the amount of trust that your horse has, the "Bow" can happen quickly or over an extended period of time. Although it is important to move at a pace that is comfortable for both you and your horse, it is also important to recognize when you are starting to stagnate in one spot. When you are training, make sure that you are constantly moving forward toward your goal of the "Bow." All the while I am asking Kassie to "Bow," I am offering verbal encouragement and lots of verbal praise. A consistent "GOOD GIRL" with LOTS of vocal inflection assures Kassie that she is doing the right thing. The "GOOD GIRL" comes when she has shifted back a fraction further then she did the last time I asked her to "Bow." Keep in mind that the "Bow" isn't as smooth as depicted here. There is a lot of rocking back and forth, and I let her foot down between each rock to give her a break. Remember, horses new to the "Bow" have to acclimate their muscles and tendons.

Applying quite a bit of pressure, I keep her nose tipped away from me. This will transfer the weight of her body onto the knee that is on the ground. Most people find the last four inches of the bow the most difficult to attain - it seems as though it is easy to focus on the end result of the knee on the ground. In truth, the last four inches are the most important. At this point, the horse is at his most precarious position and must feel that he is never going to touch the ground. Most horses will blow out of the "Bow" in the last four inches. Now you can release the foot a couple of times to let him know that the ground is near. After those couple of times, however, use a lot of praise and vocal inflection to encourage your horse to come all the way to the ground. Compare the two styles of training. Notice that there is less physical strain on my back with the aid of the two ropes compared to when I used no mechanical aid. Kassie is unconcerned with either method.

Comfortable with the "Bow," I will let the pressure off the halter rope just enough to let Kassie tuck her nose. When you are just starting you can help hold the "Bow" by dropping the ropes and quickly feeding treats to your bowing horse. You should only feed treats like this once or twice though, as the horse might start to 'grab and run'. The reward should come after you give a verbal release to your horse, not at the point when he hits the ground with this knee. For more head-strong horses, use the ropes to balance between the "Bow" and lifting up out of it. Playing with the pressure on each rope will allow you to determine how much pull is required to ease your horse into the "Bow", and then keep him there. Remember, you don't want your horse to pop up as soon as he feels the release of the ropes. This is when telling your horse to "Hold" is most important. Your horse should listen to you for the retention and release of the "Bow," and not the release of the physical restraints.

After being relaxed in the "Bow" for even just a second, all pressure is released and THEN I tell her "UP." Initially, don't keep your horse in a "Bow" for more than a second or so as you don't want to strain muscles or tendons. If your horse blows up before you release him, then you may have held him down for too long. Training the "Bow" is the beginning of intense communication between you and your horse. He will be speaking volumes to you, and it is up to you to listen. It is through the "Bow" that your horse will learn to trust you enough for the "Kneel" and the "Lie-Down." If you don't pay attention to what your horse is telling you, achieving the "Lie-Down" will be difficult at best. Training the "Bow" is finding your own personal balance. You can't be too soft or your horse will learn to flail and walk all over you. Your horse won't trust someone who is too weenie to look after him. Alternatively, being overbearing won't win you any trust points either. The bow is where you start your partnership.

After Kassie comes up from the "Bow," she is rewarded with treats and praise for a job well done. Once your horse is touching the ground with his knee, I generally follow this rule of thumb. Once is lucky, twice is accidental, three times is learned. If he can "Bow" three times, call it a day. The next time out, ask for three pretty "Bows" and so on.

Keep practicing having your horse move back and down into the "Bow" until he can touch the ground with his knee. As soon as his knee touches the ground, tell your horse to "Hold" and offer him treat rewards. Don't forget to praise and give treat rewards for every small amount of 'try' that he offers. If your horse is so very near the ground but chickens out before touching, help him

98

along by letting his foot down to touch the ground. Once he knows that the ground is there, he will have the confidence to complete the "Bow." If your horse keeps his back feet too close to his front feet and runs out of bowing room, tap the cornet band of his back foot with your toe to get him to engage his hind end and step backward.

POTENTIAL PROBLEMS:

My horse was tipping his nose, but now he turns his head to the left and I can't pull it back to the right – Your horse might be getting tired, or he might be getting a little too nervous. Instead of clipping the shank to the ring under his halter, clip it to the left cheek ring which will give you better leverage in tipping his head to the left. Ask for one more attempt and end the session for the day. In your last attempt, let your horse's foot touch the ground so that he knows that the ground is near. He is worried that he is going to fall down and probably needs a little more support and encouragement from you.

My horse leaned back a couple of times but now he flails around and tries to jerk his foot free – your horse might need to be handled a little more to gain more confidence and trust in you. Alternatively, this might be a dominance issue where your horse doesn't feel the need to participate. You can either shelve teaching the "Bow" for now and do some more ground work with your horse to establish a more trusting relationship, or you can work through the problem until you get past this barrier and continue with the "Bow." Beware that if you do decide to work through the problem, you will be dealing with a relatively unimpressed horse. Expect your horse to try to walk away on three legs, lunge around, and just generally be belligerent. If you decide to start this battle of wills, then be prepared to see it through to the end. If your horse wins you may never be able to achieve the "Bow" because your horse will have learned to out-muscle you. If you find yourself in a contest of strength, then I recommend incorporating the use of the running "V," which will give you the upper hand and help see you through to the end in one piece. At this point, don't worry about your horse, he is just toying with you. If you really decide that having a "Bowing" horse is worth it at this point, then worry about how you are going to protect yourself. Before you decide to commit to a "Battle Royale", seriously think about whether or not you can commit the time to training the "Bow." If your horse shows resistance, you will have to be prepared to commit ½ hour a day for a *minimum* of 30 days. If you can't commit to this time, then you are going to repeat the fight over and over and over.

My horse lost his balance and is lying on the ground – Not a big deal, he's just moved onto the next trick unexpectedly fast! If you horse winds up on the ground stay calm. Pet him and tell him to relax. You can feed him treats, or ease his head over so that he is lying flat. You could get him up right away, but you will be training him to "Lie-Down" soon enough. As this is his first experience with the 'requested' "Lie-Down," make the experience as pleasant and relaxing as possible. If your horse stays down for ½ hour, then so be it! Continue to pet him and talk to him. Let him fall asleep if he wants. When he decides to get up, just continue with "Bowing." If your horse is super trusting and wants to "Lie-Down" all the time, then you are really lucky! Remind him that you are asking for just a "Bow" by spurring him in the belly with something blunt – like the handle of a hoof-pick. I know that this sounds a little harsh, but for some reason when a horse is bent on lying down, it takes a pretty strong reminder for him to stay upright. This is the same if your horse tries to "Bow" while you are working with his feet. A firm reminder in the belly will keep him standing properly instead of falling down on top of you or your farrier. Once you have your horse "Bowing," it's time to start removing the ropes that helped you get there. Refer to <u>Finishing the Bow</u> at the end of this section for the final steps in the bow sequence.

3. TEACHING THE BOW USING A RUNNING "V"

As with the previous two methods, "Bowing" with the help of the running "V" (or a version of it anyway) requires that you have soft, deep ground, a bucket of treats, and protective wrapping on your horse's legs. This method will also require 3 lead ropes, a halter and a single hock hobble. After reading the first two methods you may choose to use the running V right off the bat, or you might want to try your hand with the other two options first. The decision is up to you. The running V just allows you to better manage the weight of your horse, but the concept of the bow remains the same.

The first lead rope will run from your horse's halter, along the left side of his neck and over his withers – by pulling this rope you will be able to tip his nose away from you, to the left. Tie the second lead rope (a long, thick, cotton lead shank works best) around his girth. Thread the rope in a lasso type fashion so that when the end of the rope is pulled, it tightens around the girth. Snug the rope around the girth (it's no worse than a saddle being cinched up) and tie the end off so that the rope doesn't come loose. Snap your third rope to the bottom of the rope that runs around the girth. The third rope should now be hanging straight down behind your horses front legs. Place the hock hobble around the ankle of your horse's right front leg, and thread the end of the third rope through the large ring of the hock hobble. When you hold the end of the third rope up, it will resemble a "V".

Tap your horse's shoulder and ask him to give you his foot. When he shifts his weight, pull straight up on the third rope to pick up his foot. If he doesn't shift his weight, tap his cannon bone or his cornet band with your toe (you don't have to tap hard, just bump him to encourage him to pick up his foot). Hold his leg up so that his cannon bone is running parallel to the ground. There is no reason to wrench his foot up so high that his knee points down.

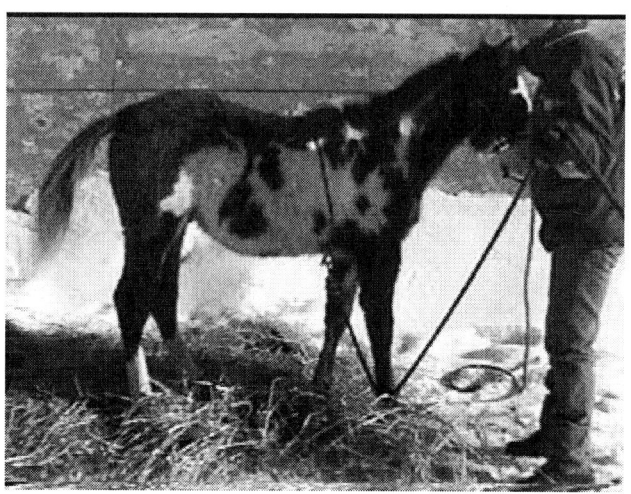

A Running 'V' is called this because of it's 'V' shape. The rope that I am holding snaps onto a separate rope tied around Duster's girth. It runs from the clip to the single hobble around his 'ankle'.

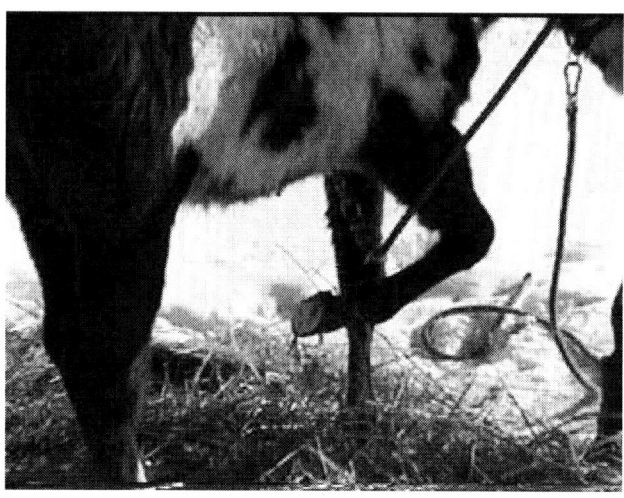

At the same time I ask Duster to pick up his foot, I will keep tension on the Running 'V' rope. This mechanism allows me to hold much of his weight using very little force.

After picking up Duster's foot using the Running 'V', I tip his nose away from me by pulling on the lead rope that is snapped to his halter.

As he leans backward I reduce the amount of pressure applied to his halter rope. I want to apply enough pressure to keep him leaning backwards, but not enough to keep his nose tipped so far away from me. Tipping a horse's nose too far to the side for the duration of the bow will cause him to lose his balance completely and fall.

When Duster is solid on the ground, I will release the tension on the Running 'V' rope and the halter rope. Telling Duster to 'Hold' I will re-apply tension to the ropes if he shows signs of trying to get up before I give him the cue 'UP!'. Confident that he is relaxed in the "Bow," I release the ropes completely and give Duster a scratch, and a treat, to encourage him to relax in the bow.

The ropes released, I tell Duster 'UP'. The session depicted here is the 3rd "Bowing" session where I have used the Running "V" on this colt. This mechanical aid is a very direct approach to teaching the "Bow". Although you can expect some resistance (such as hopping around) at the start of training, you don't want to frighten your horse to the point of rearing. Training the "Bow" isn't a test of strength, for you will surely lose. Rather, it is a meeting of minds - it is through training the bow that you will discover exactly the type of relationship that you have with your horse. If the relationship that you have with your equine companion is one of trust and respect, then you will achieve the "Bow" without much difficulty. If you discover that your horse is defying you outright during this training, then it's time to seriously assess whether or not you really are the respected leader in your horse's eyes. Should you find yourself lacking, it's time to review your basic horsemanship skills.

Have your horse stand quietly a few seconds before you release his foot back to the ground. Once your horse is comfortable having his foot picked up in this manner, tap his shoulder again and lift his foot off the ground.

Once again, you find yourself with two options. You can entice your horse to lean back by drawing him down onto his leg with his treat reward, or you can tip his nose to the left and use the shifting of his weight to bring him down and back into the bow. I stress that, as with the other methods, you must reward subtle shifting and 'try'. Using the Running "V" is not a down and dirty quick fix. You must still follow all the praise and reward of the previous two methods. What the Running "V" does, is give your horse a greater sense of security because you can 'float' his weight better as opposed to trying to hold his foot up with one hand and reach a treat out to him with the other (which causes his leg to twist and his weight to shift).

Once you have your horse touching the ground with his right leg, you can use the Running "V" arrangement to better hold him in position. Keeping the rope of the Running "V" snug, and his nose tipped to the left makes it possible but difficult for him to rise from the bow. The more you tip his nose, the more weight you put onto his tethered leg. At this point, it is possible to overdo it and tumble your horse onto the ground so be aware of this and learn to read him so that you don't shift his weight too much. When your horse is in the "Bow", release all ropes and tell him "Up". The Running "V" will automatically loosen, and your horse will be able to move freely until you pick up the end of the third rope again.

When your horse is able to perform a "Bow" smoothly off the tap from his shoulder (you will still have to support his leg for a while), remove all the ropes and back to method 2. Bowing With the Help of Simple Mechanical Aids. Once your horse has the idea planted firmly in his mind, you no longer require the use of ropes and hock hobbles.

The most common problem is blowing out of the "Bow." In this photo, we can see the effectiveness of the Running "V." Haley attempts to evade Brenda's request by lunging upwards. With the assistance of the running V, Brenda is able to hold Haley into a bow while she still remains in an upright position, safe from the lunging Haley. You can see from Haley's expression that she doesn't feet threatened by the direct approach of the running V, and the fact that the rope to her halter is slack tells us that she is familiar with the "Bow." The extra lead rope has just been looped around her neck to get it out of the way. This mare is so familiar with the "Bow" that Brenda is actually cueing her to lean back by applying pressure to the rope looped loosely around her neck. The reason the Running "V" was incorporated at this point was because the mare learned that she didn't have to stay in the bow, and was popping up . Brenda uses the Running "V" to regain control of this trick.

A nice controlled "Bow." From this angle you can see how the Running "V" works with the belly rope to keep control of the "Bow." Brenda is just about to feed Haley her treat reward and give her the verbal command of 'UP as she releases the ropes of the Running "V." In this one, short session, Haley learned not to evade Brenda's "Bowing" request. Had Brenda allowed her to continue evading the "Bow" in it's proper form, Haley would have become inconsistent and disrespectful with the "Bow" as she started to lose respect for Brenda At that time, any chance Brenda had for progressing beyond the "Bow" would have been lost. You can see from Haley's ears that, although she is thougful of the correction, she is not distressed or angry. Experience and a strong relationship with your horse will tell you when your horse starts to evade your training requests and begins to lose respect for you.

FINISHING THE BOW

After much practice, your horse will start to shift his weight, or pick up his foot when you tap his shoulder. When you pick up his foot he will start to lean back immediately. There are two things for you to do now; get him to hold the "Bow" for an extended period of time and stop picking up his foot – he should be able to do that himself.

Start by getting your horse to hold the "Bow." What easier way to do this than with food! When your horse gets his knee on the ground, tell him "HOLD!" and shove a bucket full of treats or oats in front of his face so that he will have a good reason to stay down there. While he is happily munching away for a few seconds, stand up and ask him to rise from the bow. He has some muscles and tendons that need to stretch out so don't ask him to stay down too long at first and be understanding if he shows discomfort – this is all new to him! Once he is comfortable with holding the "Bow," don't offer the treat reward any more. Ask him for the "Bow," and have him stay there. If he tries to get up, scold him and put him back into the "Bow." Once he is "Bowing" tell him to "HOLD". After a few seconds, ask him to rise up and then give him his treat reward.

After your horse has learned to hold the "Bow" until you tell him to rise, it's time to make the "Bow" pretty. Start to get your horse listening to the shoulder cue and instead of picking his foot up, guide his foot back to the "Bow" position by tapping his cannon bone with your toe or the handle of a short whip. Over time, minimize his reliance on your toe to guide his foot back. If he is sluggish in moving his foot back, give him a firm tap on his cannon bone. Your horse knows what to do, he just has to learn to accept responsibility in carrying out this trick.

My cue for Reamo is on his shoulder. This cue placement becomes important for the riding "Bow," where I will use my heel to trigger the "Bow" response.

Tapping Reamo's shoulder, I ask him to "Bow". Reamo responds by lifting his foot....

..... and shifting backward

109

When a horse is at the beginning of the finished "Bow," use your toe to help guide his foot back and down. This little bit of help prevents frustration and confusion for both you and your horse. It isn't long before you won't need to help him place his foot.

Reamo completes the "Bow" by resting his knee on the ground. Once your horse becomes smooth in the "Bow" from a ground cue, it's time to move to the riding "Bow."

Without any riding aids, I am using my heel on Reamo's shoulder to cue the "Bow."

THE RIDING BOW

Requirements: Long whip, protective knee/leg wrap, soft ground, treats reward.

While sitting on your horse, lean back and bump his right shoulder with your right heel. Your horse will "Bow."

When your horse is rock solid in the "Bow" you can start to ask for a riding "Bow". In order to get the riding "Bow," he must be able to "Bow" from the ground with only the shoulder cue and no additional assistance from you. It is more difficult for the horse to execute the riding "Bow" because of the balance involved. Add the continually shifting weight of a rider and the degree of difficulty increases. In light of this, it is very important to sit still while your horse is "Bowing."

While sitting on your horse, lean back and bump his right shoulder with your heel. Tell your horse to "Bow." Your horse might attempt to "Bow," he might start to back up or he might not do anything at all. If your horse attempts the "Bow," reward him! If he starts to back up or just stands there, use the long whip to tap his cannon bone while you are cueing his shoulder with your heel. Just like teaching the Spanish walk, transferring to the saddle just takes a little time because you are changing your position, which changes the cue dramatically. This is another trick where your horse will tell you if he is ready or not. It is very important to reward 'try' in the riding "Bow." If your horse goes only so far as to lower his head; for example, you must reward the try with praise and treat, then use the whip to tap his cannon bone to further clarify your command. Your horse has a good understanding of what you want, he just has to figure out how to get himself there.

When starting the riding "Bow," I helped Reamo to understand what I wanted by using his halter shank against his neck and tapping his shoulder with my heel. Using the lead shank to tip his nose away from his bent leg goes back to our initial stages of training the "Bow." All we are doing is transferring the cue from a ground cue to a riding cue. When transferring cues, don't expect that your horse should know what you want. Help him along by using familiar aids. It is important to sit solid when requesting the riding "Bow." Wiggling around will throw him off balance and might make him reluctant to "Bow." You should also be prepared in case he accidentally falls or decides to lie down.

KNEEL

Requirements: Soft ground, protective leg wraps, treat reward
Prerequisite: Bow
Watch Out For: Lunging horse, horse off balance.

While your horse is in a "Bow," ask him to kneel by telling him "Other Foot."

While you were teaching him to "Bow," your horse might have discovered that it is easier to tuck both his front legs underneath him, than it is to keep one stuck straight out. If he hasn't learned this yet then you can help him along. When your horse can "Bow," and hold the "Bow" until you ask him to rise, you can request that he tuck his other foot to get a kneel. When your horse is bowing, reach under his neck with a short crop (or your toe if you are agile enough) and tell your horse "Other Foot". In response to the tapping on his cannon bone, he will tuck his other foot underneath his chest. With practice, you will be able to just tell your horse "Other Foot" and he will go from bowing to kneeling.

A lot of people have trouble achieving the kneel, and some have no problems at all. One of the most important aspects of the kneel is the relationship that you have with your horse. Before attempting the kneel, you must ensure that your horse is rock solid in his "Bow." This means when you request the "Bow," he can hold the position until you tell him "Up." When you can do this then you have the bow down pat and you should be able to achieve the kneel without any problems.

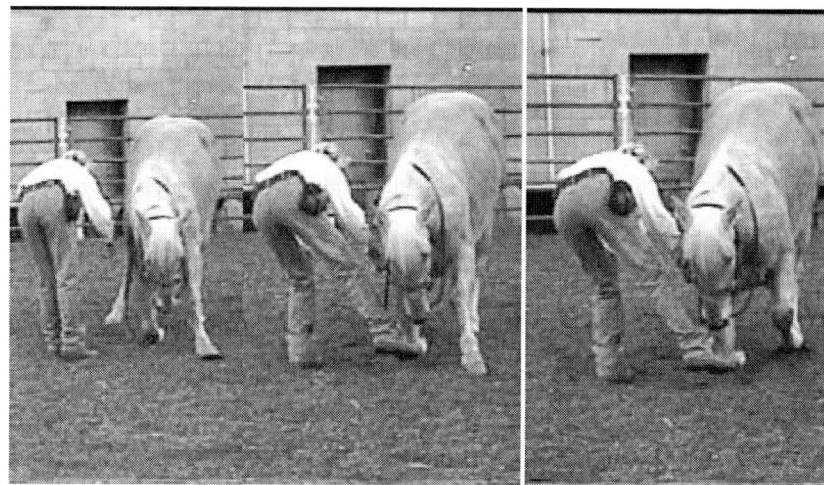

When Reamo is "Bowing" (top left), I tap his cannon bone with my toe, or whip if you prefer, (top middle) to encourage him to tuck his leg (top right) and kneel (bottom). After only a few repetitions, you only need to point to his outstretched leg and tell him "Other foot!" and he will tuck his extended leg and kneel.

Another view of the kneel. I ask Reamo to "Bow" by tapping his shoulder (left). When his knee is solid on the ground, I tell him 'other foot' while continuing to tap his shoulder. You can see that, from my verbal cue, Reamo is tucking his extended leg. As you practice, it will no longer be necessary to physically cue the extended leg. A verbal cue and tapping on his shoulder are sufficient.

While I continue to tap his shoulder, Reamo continues to tuck his leg (left) until he is kneeling(right). At this time I cease tapping and offer him his reward. Once your horse is bowing, you can teach him how to crawl. However, you may prefer to teach the "Lie-Down" first and come back to the crawl. The reason you might want to bypass crawl for now is that your horse is getting used to you requesting 'downward motion'. Teaching the crawl at this point might ruin this momentum and make teaching the "Lie-Down" more difficult.

Using a halter and lead rope to encourage forward movement, Reamo follows me at a crawl.

CRAWL

Requirements: Halter and lead rope, protective leg/knee wraps, treat reward.
Prerequisite: Bow and Kneel
Watch Out For: Front feet striking out if horse jumps up.

While your horse is kneeling, take his lead rope in your hand and, while crawling in front of him, tell him to "Crawl". Your horse will crawl along behind you.

Training your horse to crawl is a little like training him to lead all over again. In this session you will have to, once again, reward 'try'. While your horse is kneeling, tug on his lead rope and tell him "Crawl". If your horse shows any indication that he wants to move forward, tell him he is good and reward him. The only caution is to watch that he doesn't inadvertently teach himself camel stretch (detailed next). Although it is great to reward forward movement of the head and neck in the primary stages of crawling, the real reward should come when he moves his front legs forward.

If your horse moves one front leg slightly, pet the leg that is doing well, tell him that he is good, and provide him his treat reward. Ask for a little more and a little more so that he takes one crawling step, then two, etc. Soon he will be crawling behind you. If he tries to extend his front foot too much when you are asking for a crawl, tap his cannon bone to get him to re-tuck the foot and continue with training.

It is most important that you have sufficient protective padding on his knees and shins for this trick. Your horse will be dragging his knees and grinding his shins into the dirt. Any discomfort or damage that he receives will cause him to resist.

CAMEL STRETCH

Requirements: Protective leg/knee wraps, treat reward.
Prerequisite: Bow and Kneel.

When your horse is kneeling, tell him to "Stretch". Your horse will stretch his neck out in front of him and rest his head and neck on the ground.

While your horse is kneeling, squat down near his head and entice him with a treat reward. Use the treat to encourage him to stretch out his neck. When he has stretched his neck out to the furthest that he can stretch it, praise him and give him his treat reward. Finish the camel stretch by reducing his reliance on the treat reward as bait to stretch. Ask him to reach his head forward to your fingers and then give him the treat reward after he has finished and returned to his feet. Over time, reduce the need for your fingers as an additional cue until he can stretch his neck out at your verbal command.

Reamo is solid in his kneel. I can now encourage him to stretch out his neck by baiting him with treats.

LIE-DOWN

Requirements: Two lead ropes, protective leg/knee wraps, halter, treat reward.
Prerequisite: "Bow" and "Kneel."
Watch Out For: Falling horse, horse rapidly rising, horse rolling.

After asking your horse to "Bow," then "Kneel," continue to tap his shoulder and tell him "Down." Your horse will ease himself into a "Lie-Down."

There are 2 ways that I teach the "Lie-Down." The first method is just to wait the horse out and, on his own he will get bored of the kneel and decide that it takes less effort to just "Lie-Down.". A horse will generally indicate that he has the desire to "Lie-Down" when he stretches his head and neck out in the camel stretch while he is kneeling. Some horses are awkward and unsure of themselves and seem to get 'stuck' in the camel stretch. Or, they might have surprised themselves when they first attempted the "Lie-Down" and are now hesitant. Your horse will tell you when he is ready to "Lie-Down", all you have to do is listen.

If your horse happens to get 'stuck' in the camel stretch, you can help him achieve the 'down'. Tie a long cotton lead shank around his girth. Thread the rope in a lasso type fashion so that when the end of the rope is pulled, it tightens around the horses girth. While you are pulling the end of the rope, tell him "Down". Be careful if you decide to ease your horse into the "Lie-Down" as they often take on a 'timber' appearance and kind of roll over their shoulder rather stiff legged. When he is on the ground let him relax and get his bearings back. Feed him lots of treats and tell him he is wonderful. When he lays down for you, he is displaying a lot of trust in you – it is now your responsibility not to betray that trust by ensuring that nothing bad happens to him while he is on the ground. Ease his head onto your lap and let him relax – he might even fall asleep! When he displays signs that he is ready to get back up, step out of his way and tell him "Up." Rest a few minutes and ask him to "Lie-Down" again. As you practice more and more your horse will buckle his back legs and "Lie-Down" easily rather then tumble down.

The rope on his girth isn't meant to toss your horse onto the ground, it's just meant to ease him down so that you can show him that there is an easier place to be. If your horse really resists your attempts to lie him down, you may be moving a little too fast for him. If he even makes a downward attempt (ie. folds his legs a little more and lowers his chest), then reward the 'try' and let him relax before asking him to come down further. As with all the tricks, you gain milestones by millimeters when asking your horse to "Lie-Down.".

Once your horse learns to "Lie-Down" from pressure applied to his girth, it's time to transfer the cue somewhere else. If you are going to ask him to "Lie-Down" while you're riding him, then it's handy to have two cues at the same time. Run a lead rope from his halter, down the left side of his neck. At the same time that you are applying pressure to the girth rope, tug gently on the rope running to the halter and tell him "Down". Your

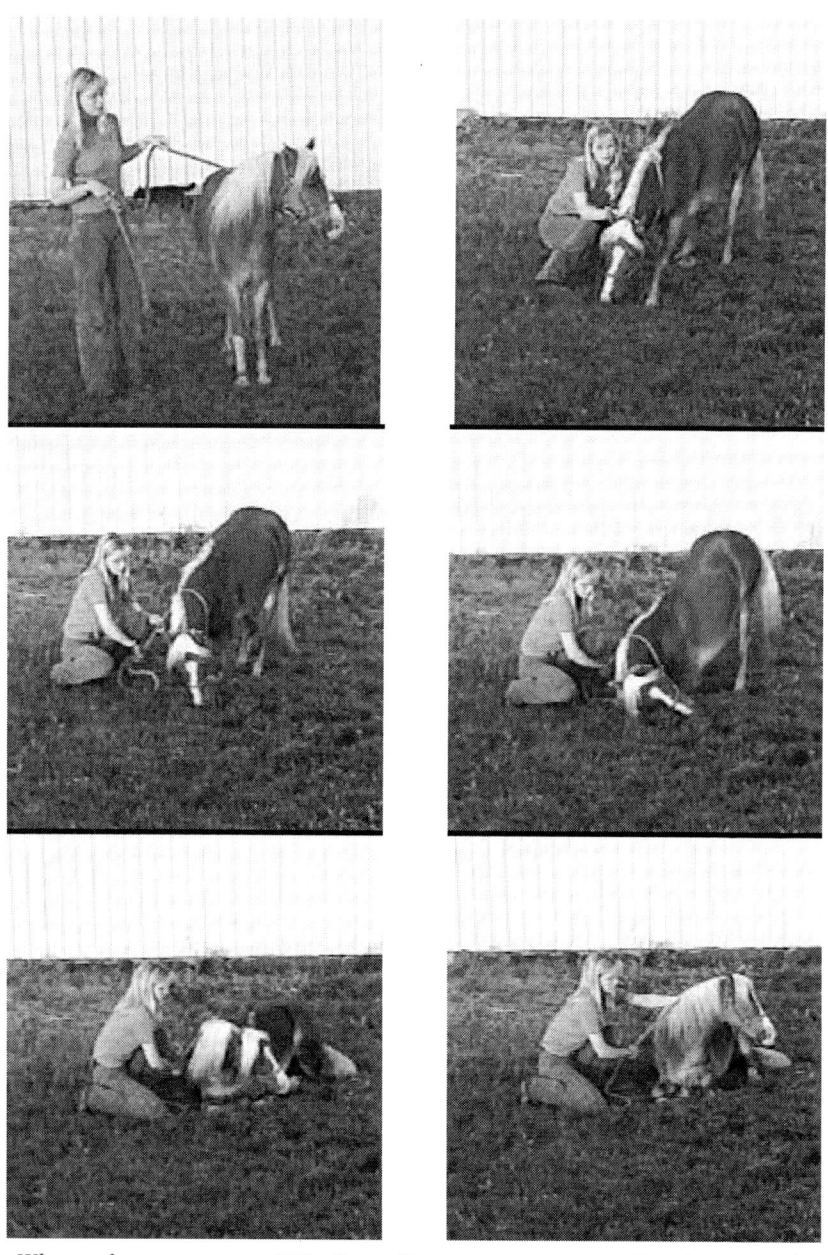

When a horse starts to "Lie-Down," you can encourage him by using the lead rope to tip his nose away from you. In this sequence we see "Nugget' the Shetland, "Lie-Down" as I use the lead rope to tip his nose and draw him down. As a caution, when starting out, many horses will kind or roll over their shoulder and almost somersault. You must always be aware!

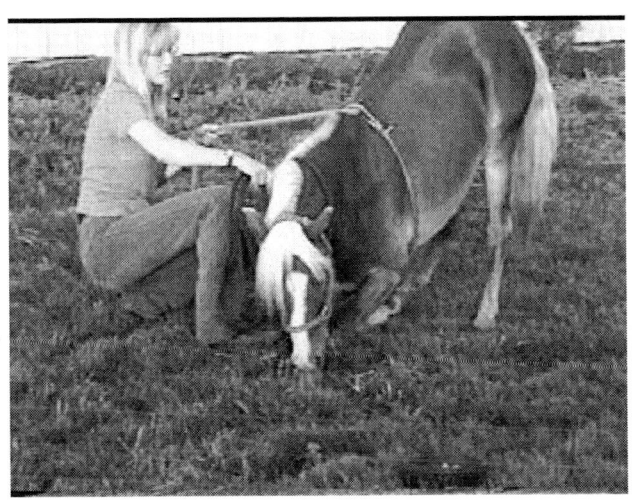

If your horse gets 'stuck' in the kneel, use a rope around his girth to draw him down. I have run my lead rope through the snap so that the more I pull it, the more snug it becomes around Nugget's girth.

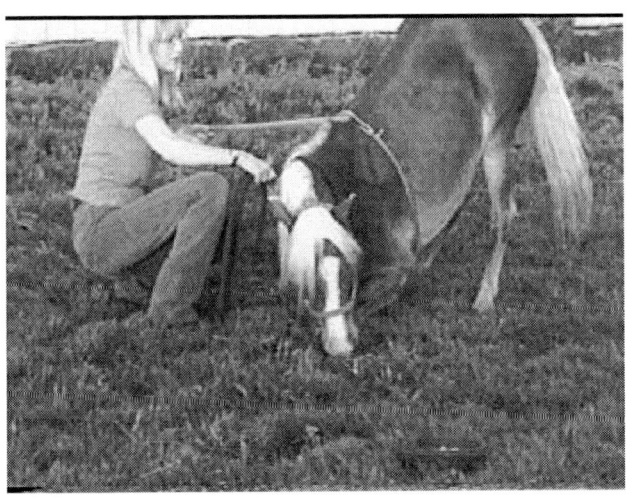

A subtle shift. Nugget lowers himself a fraction. This attempt must be rewarded with exhuberant "GOOD BOY's". By now, Nugget has learned that GOOD BOY means that he is doing what I ask. You can see that I have released tension on the rope a bit to acknowledge that sinking down is the right move.

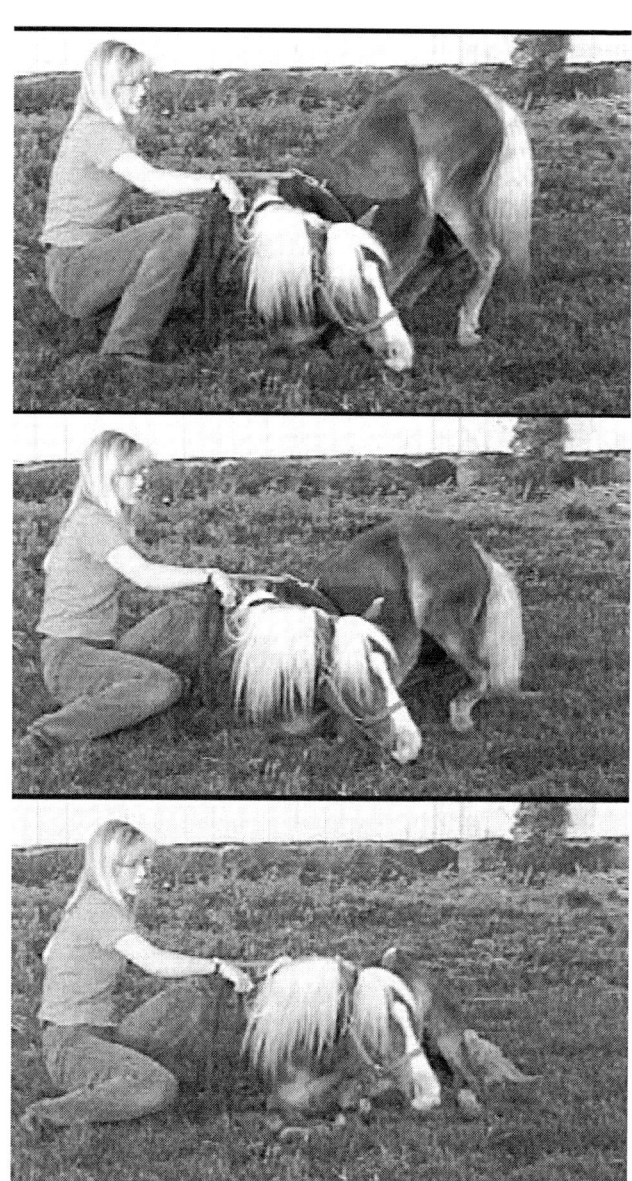

While continuing to apply pressure on the girth rope, I gently tip Nugget's nose away from me. His response is to relax his hind end and complete the "Lie-Down." You must be tactful when doing this. If you use too much force you will pull your horse over in a somersault on top of yourself. Ensure your guidance with the rope is smooth. It's a balancing act and you don't want to tip the scales (or the horse) on top of you.

goal is to transfer the cue from the girth rope to the rope running to your horse's halter. When you have eliminated the need for the rope around the girth, ask him for a "Bow," then use the rope running to his halter to request the 'down'. If you would like to refine your cue further, you can have him "Bow" and "Lie-Down" off the shoulder cue by transferring the "Lie-Down" cue from the halter rope, to the shoulder.

At this point you are probably wondering why you just wouldn't transfer the cue from the girth rope to the shoulder. You can do this without a problem! The reason that I use the additional step of a halter cue is so that I have a backup if my horse has a memory lapse in the middle of a demonstration. If I cue for the "Bow," then continue to the "Lie-Down" using the shoulder cue, and he ignores the cue, I immediately reinforce the shoulder cue with the halter (or bridle) cue. It's a quick disciplinary fix that the audience won't notice and it's much more subtle than the rope around the girth.

Now that you have a solid "Lie-Down" cue, and your horse lies down quietly and is happy to stay down, you can request the "Lie-Down" while sitting on your horse. Cue him for the "Bow" and give the additional cue for the down. If he pops out of the "Bow," cue it again and use the halter/rope backup cue to tip his nose thus shifting his weight for the "Lie-Down." Once he is lying down, let him relax.

Now, you have the opportunity to learn from my mistakes! While attending a horse show, I had just finished a rather intense warm up session when someone yelled at me, "Lie your horse down". Now, I must say that I knew the gal who issued the request and to this day I don't believe that she has a devious bone in her body. Not one to disappoint I had my horse at the time "Lie-Down" - only to have him start to roll....ON MY NEW SADDLE! So beware of the "Lie-Down"...if you aren't paying attention, it might be hard on your equipment!

The sequence of the "Riding Down". After asking for a "Bow," I have asked Reamo to tuck his 'other foot' using a verbal cue. I then give him the verbal cue of "Down". (You will notice that I am not working in the best ground.) My relationship with Reamo is such that he trusts me enough to "Lie-Down" on any ground surface – a trust that should not be abused. Although it is difficult to tell from the photograph, when Reamo is lying flat, I am not sitting on him with my full weight.

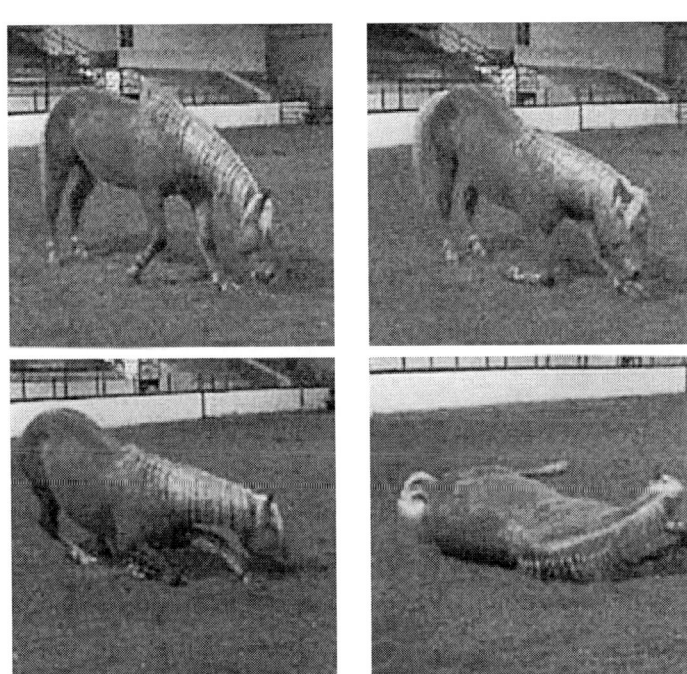

"Bow" and "Lie-Down" at liberty. Reamo demonstrates this trick at a clinic. I am a few feet in front of him cueing with a long whip. Start the liberty "Bow" and/or down by standing in front of your horse and tapping his shoulder with a long whip while telling him 'Bow'. With practice, you will be able to move farther and farther away.

After finishing the "Lie-Down" at liberty, Reamo performs a liberty sit. I am cueing from a short distance away.

SIT UP

Requirements: Lots of treat reward.
Prerequisite: Bow, Kneel and "Lie-Down."
Watch Out For: Rapidly rising horse.

While your horse is lying down, walk around the front of him and over to his left-hand side. Snap your fingers in the air above his head and tell your horse to "Sit". Your horse will lift his front end and, using his front feet, push himself up into a sit.

The sit is easy to teach your horse as long as you have timing and patience. When he goes from a "Lie-Down" to a stand, there are 3 steps (presuming he doesn't decide to get up hind end first like a cow). Generally, horses will "Lie-Down" on their right hip – this is why you trained your horse to "Bow" and "Lie-Down" on the right hand side (if your horse is a lefty I hope that you have been accommodating him so far). When getting up they will extend their left front leg, then their right front leg and rise. Essentially, the extension of the two front legs allows you two chances to stop him before he is standing on all four feet.

He should be extremely comfortable in the "Lie-Down" before you move on to the "Sit Up." Ask him to "Sit" and as soon as he extends the left front leg, stuff a bucket full of goodies in front of his nose. Allow him to sit like this and eat for a few seconds. Use your toe or a riding crop to tap his right front leg and encourage him to extend it. Be careful because he might decide that this dog-like position is just too awkward and lurch up. Tell him he is good, keep him calm and quiet, and ask him to "Lie-Down" again. Once again, ask him to rise but thwart his attempts by appealing to his stomach. Soon, your horse will learn to appreciate the mobile buffet and will sustain the front-feet-forward "Lie-Down.". The next step is to get him pushing himself back and up with his front feet.

You can encourage him to move his front feet back by tapping his cornet band with your toe and telling him "Sit". Reward little steps with praise and cookies. Encourage him to "Hold" his position and continue to reward him with food.

Using a halter rope and belly rope Spike has learned to go into the "Lie-Down" with little resistance. I am feeding him biscuits to keep him comfortable and content in the down.

Comfortable with the "Lie-Down," 'Spike' has perfected the first stage of sitting. To encourage him to stay in this stretched out pose, I am feeding a lot of treats. Initially, a belly rope was used to ease 'Spike' into the down.

As your horse demonstrates his desire to stay in this goofy, outstretched, pose, there is no longer any need to use the food bucket. Instead, feet him treat by treat as you encourage him to push his front feet back more and more.

If his feet stay rock solid in front of him, you can encourage the movement by holding a treat near the left side of his belly (where his legs are). In his attempt to reach the treat, he will try to walk with his front feet. Reward him with praise, treats, and pet the front legs. Over time, encouragement will have him sitting like a dog. He will start by lifting his brisket off the ground. From there you can encourage him to move higher and higher by tapping his cornet band and telling him "Bigger". Keep rewarding 'try' and soon he will be sitting to his maximum height.

The belly rope no longer needed, Spike, rewarded with a treat, is hlding the sit.

Move in small steps. Once he has one leg out in front of him, quit for the day or for a while. The next session, ask him to stick both front legs out, and then end the session again. Once he has stuck both front legs out in front of him, the hard part is over and the next step is just getting him to walk back with his front legs. If he makes any movement back with his front leg (s), pet the 'good' leg and praise him. Soon, your horse will discover that walking up with his front legs puts him into a more comfortable position than with his legs stretched out like a dog.

Getting out of a full sit up can be awkward at first so when you ask your horse to get up, step clear so that he doesn't stumble into you. With time and practice he will become more graceful in this maneuver.

A nice, finished, sit. After being placed in the sit without any additional aids, Spike can now be left in the sit position until cued to rise up. We placed him beside this jump to display the height of the obstacle that he was previously jumping. The jump has no bearing on the sit.

Potential Problems:

My horse can stretch his front legs out with no problem but he keeps lurching up - Training this way doesn't get the sit up all in one shot, you build height gradually. At first, your horse might only raise his brisket off the ground an inch or two but you keep encouraging to get the height over time. If he shows signs of trying to lurch up, tell him to 'whoa' and 'hold' and stop the action by stuffing food in front of his face. It also helps to have a word that signifies that you are looking for more effort - like 'bigger'.... Which says, "keep doing what you are doing but do more of it."

Lurching up the first few times can be expected but the horse begins to understand that he can expend less energy and consume more food if he just stays in the sit. You are rewarding the fraction of a second that he stayed in the sit, the getting up and chewing is incidental.

When it came time to illustrate the sit, I quickly realized that I had overtrained 'Spike' (who was going to be my book horse). By the time we were ready for photos he was too good at sitting and needed only a snap of the fingers as a cue. As luck would have it, I stumbled across a video that I did of 'Nugget' (an est. 6-8 year old Shetland). In the first two pictures, 'Nugget' is assuming the Sphinx position by outstretching first one front leg, then the other. I am snapping my fingers in the first picture to encourage him to outstretch his front legs. As soon as he puts the second leg forward, I stuff treats at him, causing him to stop any thoughts about rising.

In these photos I am actually holding my treat hand a little too high. I should have my hand near his belly which will cause him to attempt to walk around with his front legs to reach the cookies. However, 'Nugget' is a little sluggish and I am using my other hand to lift him up by his halter. 'Nugget' was sold before I had the chance to complete the polished sit up.

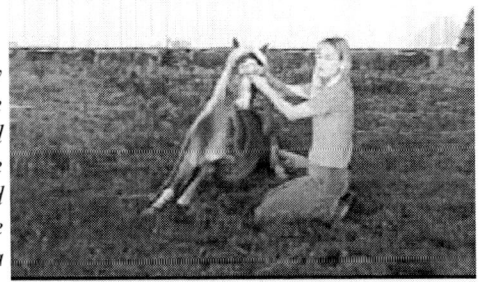

Nugget (above) is in the middle of learning his sit up. By using treats I encourage him to hold the sit before giving him a verbal cue to stand. Over time, I would have practiced him sitting up higher and higher until he had reached his full sit height.

Imagine my surprise when I discovered that Spike (my 'book' pony) had been too thoroughly trained!

THE REAR

THINK HARD BEFORE YOU TEACH THIS!

Training the Ground Rear and the Riding Rear is a continuous training circle. If you decide to teach both styles of rear, then each is dependent on the other when it comes to training. Once you begin training the rear, you have it for life. Before you commit to any rearing, seriously consider whether or not you can provide the discipline required to keep you and your horse safe. Consider, also whether or not you are going to keep your horse for life, or only for a couple of years. Once you train the rear on any level, you have the responsibility to your horse to ensure that all future owners are aware of and trained in the rear – including the disciplinary requirements.

THE RIDING REAR

Requirements: Saddle, bridle, treat reward.
Watch Out For: You are teaching your horse to rear - watch out for everything! The riding rear may interfere with your horse backing up. You must practice the riding rear and the back up to help your horse distinguish between the two.
Prerequisite: Your horse should be well trained for riding. He should be calm and obedient while under saddle. You must be able to discipline your horse if he offers you a riding rear uninvited.

Tell your horse "Ready?" while you jiggle the reins. Apply pressure with your legs and pull back with your reins while at the same time, tell your horse "UP!" Your horse will rear. As soon as you feel the horse start to lift off the ground, release all pressure on your reins and legs.

My horses have 5 cues (both verbal and physical) that, when

combined, will produce a riding rear. I have used five cues so that someone who has no clue what they are doing can't (hopefully) stumble upon the riding rear. There are two ways that you can teach the riding rear: either in conjunction with the ground rear, or independent of the ground rear. Let's look first at teaching the riding rear independent of the ground rear.

Basically, you are going to frustrate your horse to the point of blow up then reward him when he acts on this. I could flower it up and make the process sound a little more user-friendly, but, in plain English, this is what you are going to do. If you are teaching the *Ground* Rear, I can't stress enough that you DO NOT train the horse to rear out of frustration. The *Riding* Rear, however, does just that and this is how I justify it. While riding our horses we do a lot of things that frustrate them. If you have ever had a horse buck, bolt or act unexpectedly when you are trying to teach him something, then you have already frustrated a horse to the point of blow up – the initial reaction of the riding rear is just one more speed bump toward a learned behavior.

Choose a nice, quiet, spot with no distractions. Apply forward leg pressure and backward rein pressure at the same time, and, in an energetic voice command "UP!". He won't have a clue what just happened, and will be left wondering why he was just assaulted in this manner. Pat him on the neck and repeat the request. You are now going to see him start to think through the two conflicting cues. The leg pressure tells him forward, but the rein pressure tells him to move backwards. Your horse must remain calm while you are training the rear. You want him to get annoyed enough to finally rear, but you don't want his head to blow up in the process. If he's dancing around and getting more hyper by the second, stop your requests for the rear and just take a walk around to give him a chance to cool down.

Apply leg pressure and rein pressure again and repeat the command "Up!". Your horse will try to back up – apply more leg pressure and repeat the command "UP!". If he continues to back up, apply more leg pressure while always commanding

"UP!". If your horse tries to move forward, apply more rein pressure and command "UP!" He is probably swishing his tail like mad by this time. Release leg and rein pressure for a second, then re-apply and tell your horse "UP!" Very shortly he will try the last thing he can think of to please you and make a funny jump on his front feet. The second you feel him shifting weight to his back end and take a jump with his front feet, release all pressure and give your horse tons of praise and reward! Now that he has an inkling of what you are looking for, calm him right down. You only want him to act out of frustration once or twice and after that, it's time for him to use his brain to get the rear.

Apply leg and rein pressure and tell your horse "Up". Now that he knows what you want, he will offer the hoppy jump a little more readily. When he offers, release all pressure and give him praise and reward. He is going to start to get the hang of this really fast so it's time to start implementing the two additional security cues. This time when you ask him for the rear, allow him to prepare mentally and physically by jiggling your reins and asking "Ready?" then, apply leg and rein pressure and command "UP!" Your horse might be surprised at first but will soon learn to recognize the sequence. Once your horse understands that leg pressure, plus rein pressure followed by the verbal command of "UP" means rear then it's time to make the rear look pretty. You make the rear pretty by practicing. As you and your horse develop balance, strength and muscle, you will be able to get higher rears and sustain them for longer periods of time. Rearing involves a lot of balance. Add the instability of a rider, and the difficulty of a rear increases significantly. It will take time for him to get a lot of height in his rear, but consider this a blessing…you both need to learn how to ride the rear together.

Now for some words regarding discipline. If at ANY time (even during the initial stages of training) your horse rears without you cueing him, discipline is harsh and immediate! Discipline should be delivered to the part of the horse that is acting out of turn. In this case, your horse has to raise his head to get the impulsion necessary for the rear. If my horse offers a rear out of turn, he gets a resounding NO! and a quick swat of my hand that catches the tips of both ears. The "NO!" should not be a squeak, scream or squeal - it should be thunderous! The swat across the tip of the ears should not be a breezy flutter nor should it mimic the annoyance of a bug. It should be a snapping swat. It will do you no good to smack your horse in the rear end if he offers an uninvited rear. A smack in the rear end will drive the horse forward and add impulsion to the rear. Panicking and hauling on the reins will cause him to raise higher and higher – even to the point of falling over on top of you. You must stop the rear by stopping the upward impulsion of his head. Everything about the riding rear is serious business. If you want to accept the responsibility of owning a trained rearing horse, then you must also accept the responsibility of controlling that trained rear. If you can not provide discipline to this degree, then do not teach the riding rear.

Although the discipline remains the same, the training method can differ if you would like to explore a training alternative. Consider using a target to train your horse to rear. Read the instructions for a ground rear and incorporate the target into the training for the riding rear. Your horse will still show confusion when you apply both leg and rein pressure but the security of someone holding a flag for your horse to touch will offer him a hint as to the direction that you would like him to go. I can't provide you with specific direction when it comes to combining the ground rear and the riding rear. By now, you should have a strong line of communication with your horse, and, between the two of you, should be able to incorporate elements from both methods that will lead you to a successful rear.

The initial stages of the riding rear. In the top photo, you can see how much force I am applying to the reins. I am not jerking on the reins, simply applying consistent pressure. At the same time as I am applying pressure to the reins, I am also applying pressure with my heels. You can see Reamo's frustration in his open mouth, and wringing tail.

Reamo seeks release by offering a rear. As soon as he offers the rear, I start to release the pressure on my hands and heels. The release is Reamo's reward. Note the quiet tail and closed mouth.

The pressure of my heels and hands are completely removed as I feel Reamo raise into the rear. The reins slack, Reamo lowers himself to the ground. These three sequences happen almost simultaneously. Note that my body position stays consistent throughout. I strive to be still so that Reamo can maintain his balance without having to accommodate for me.

POTENTIAL PROBLEMS

My horse lunges forward when I ask him to rear – If your horse is leaping ahead, just offer praise instead of the treat reward to encourage your horse to work harder at the rear. Don't discourage the movement - you want to reward the try and ultimately your horse is just finding his balance. Apply more rein pressure to hold him back into the rear, and a little less leg pressure to minimize his forward impulsion.

My horse rears and gives a little buck at the same time – Your horse is having fun with the newly learned rear and might even give a little squeal. In this case, if you don't want to encourage the little buck at the end, give his bum a swat with your hand and don't treat reward his rearing effort.

A riding rear without equipment. My cue is a light tug on Reamo's mane, heel pressure and the verbal cue of 'UP!'

Reamo, a very soft natured horse, needs more practice in order to get maximum height from the ground rear. He completes his liberty rear tentatively as, I believe, he thinks that he is disrespecting me.

THE GROUND REAR

Requirements: Long whip, flag or rag, treat reward, another person, an area that is fenced off and not too large, where your horse can keep his attention focused on you.

Watch Out For: You are teaching your horse to rear while you stand on the ground in front of him…watch out for everything!

Stand facing your horse about 5 feet in front of him. Hold a long carriage whip in the air and tell your horse "UP!" Your horse will rear.

Under NO circumstances should you get your horse to rear by using force. I simply do not advocate a horse rearing at a handler out of anger, pain or frustration, for very obvious and dangerous reasons. Instead, we are going to communicate to the horse what we would like him to do, and attain the ground rear by molding his desire to please.

We start training the ground rear by teaching the horse to touch a flag or rag on a long stick, with his nose (for some of you who are more familiar, this is target training). Using your long whip as the flag handle, affix the flag or rag to the very tip of it. Hold the flagged whip near yourself and tell your horse to "Chup!" The reason that I use "Chup" is because it easily becomes "Up!" If you teach both the riding rear and the ground rear, then "Up!" is your verbal cue, but "Chup!" refers to touching the target…it will make sense shortly. While holding the flag, tell your horse "Chup", allow your horse to nuzzle all around you and don't move or say anything more while he does so. As soon as he touches the flag with his nose, give him his treat reward and lots of praise. When your horse learns that touching the flag with his nose nets him treats, start to move the flag away from yourself. Get your horse to touch the flag held to his right and left. Have him reach down to touch it, step back to touch it, reach up to touch it. After each successful touch of the flag, ensure that you give your horse lots of praise and his treat reward. Your goal is to get your horse so driven that he will do whatever is in his power to touch that flag with his nose.

When you have practiced having your horse touch the flag, make it more challenging by holding the flag up and just out of his reach. You want your horse to learn that, by lifting his front feet, he will be able to touch the flag, which will get him his food reward. If you have taught the riding rear, you can expedite the ground rear. Get on your horse and request the riding rear while holding the flag above his head at the same time. In this instance, you can minimize your leg and rein cues until he learns to rear when he receives the visual flag cue. Should you follow this route, then you will have to get him used to receiving the rear cue from the ground as he will not yet associate someone holding up a flag with rearing – this is where you will need some help. Have someone use the upraised flag to cue your horse from the ground. If he doesn't respond to the raised flag, then your established riding cues become your back up cues for this trick. Apply leg and rein pressure to get him to rear. Keep repeating the ground/flag cue (Don't forget to tell him "Chup!"). Minimize the cues that you are providing your horse while you are on his back until you provide no cue at all, and he rears when the flag is raised.

When he offers the riding rear at the flag command, then it's time to put everything together. You will need to have patience and reward 'try', because you are going to see the wheels turning in his head as he thinks this one through. Get off your horse, thank your assistant for his time, ask him to leave the practice area, and then cue the horse with the upraised flag from the ground. If he shows any indication that he is shifting his weight to the back end and lightening up his front end then give him praise. Keep asking him to "Chup". Trust that he will sort out that the upraised flag means "Rear." If your horse lifts his front feet off the ground just a couple of inches, praise and reward him as if he had done a full sized rear. As you practice over time, you can request that your horse give you a bigger attempt by telling him "Bigger". If he gives you small rear attempts and a few days have passed, withhold the treat reward and only give him praise. Make him work for the treat by putting forth more effort into his ground rear.

Reamo's first successful liberty rear. I am off camera cueing him with the upraised flag.

If you have decided against teaching your horse how to rear while under saddle, but would still like to train him to rear from the ground, it will just take a little longer. Get him really motivated to touch the flag with his nose. Have him walk a distance, step up onto his pedestal, walk through an obstacle course…anything so that he doesn't get bored with touching the flag. Before you know it, he will make the mental connection and lift his front end off the ground to reach the flag.

When your horse is rearing to touch the flag, you can remove the flag from the stick to achieve proper head position, better form and longer rear-time. Your horse now knows to touch the flag with his nose. Without the flag, he should be able to associate the raised whip with the rear. This is when you are going to change your command from "Chup" to "Up!".

Now that you know how to ask your horse for a ground rear, I can't stress enough the importance of controlling this movement. Be extremely clear on your raised whip command. If he offers the rear without your request, tell him "NO!" At this point you should know how to communicate with him well enough to determine if he is rearing to try to please you, or to be a brat. If he is rearing because he is confused and is trying to please you, offer a firm "No" and gently direct him toward what you are trying to achieve. For example, if he offers a rear while on his pedestal when you are really asking for a salute, then he just needs better direction. If, however, your horse offers the rear to be a brat, and if you feel that he is attempting to take control over you, then you must be prepared to offer strong discipline.

Don't get frustrated with this trick. If he just isn't getting it, he may have to mature (mentally and/or physically). From the very start, always keep it in the back of your mind that there are people in the world who train killer whales every day, to lift their entire bodies out of the water to touch a ball on a stick. If they can get a whale to do this, you can get your horse to do this! You might have to modify your request to better suit the communication style between you and your horse. Have patience, practice lots, and reward even the smallest advances!

POTENTIAL PROBLEMS:

My horse backs up a lot before he rears - Your horse is just trying to figure things out and set himself before he rears. If the backup becomes an evasion tactic, move to a smaller area where he doesn't have the room to back up.

My horse doesn't rear very high - Don't reward lazy attempts. Once your horse gets the idea that the upraised whip means to rear, tell him "Bigger" and only reward the rears that are complete in their effort and delivery.

So there you have it. The basics of trick training! Now that you have started you will discover that you will never finish. There are always new things to try, new ideas, new combinations…it's endless. As you go down the trick training road you are going to find that your horse knows his own tricks like yawning, sticking his tongue out and, in the case of a gelding, peeing on cue. By this time, you will have figured out some fun things that are exclusive to your horse. Just remember, it can take as little as three days to teach individual tricks, but it can take up to three years to make them look pretty.

One last thing that should be taught first but is so often over-looked, is how to load quietly into a trailer. I have never seen any books address the issue of trailer loading, and I have seen a ton of people and horses who don't do it very well at all. Once again, this style of training a horse to load might not be the absolute best method on the market today, but it is something that has never failed to work for me.

LOAD INTO TRAILER

Requirements: Halter, longe line, gloves, longe whip, splint boots, standard size horse trailer hooked onto a truck, a place to park the trailer with solid footing for your horse, oats, lukewarm water, something to eat and drink for yourself.

Watch Out For: Horse pulling back, rearing, lunging forward.

Lead your horse to the open door of a horse trailer and tell him "Step Up" or some other constant command that you prefer. Your horse steps into the trailer and stands tied while you continue on with your travelling preparations.

First of all, if you careen around corners at high speeds, slam on your brakes or accelerate like you are on a drag strip, then don't bother reading the rest of this because I don't blame your horse for not wanting to get into your trailer. I recommend that everyone take the opportunity to ride in a horse trailer just to see what it is like. Not only will you be surprised at the ride and the noise, but you will also have a new understanding of just how amazing your horse is to agree to ride in a metal box on wheels.

Now, you might be wondering how a trailer lesson fits into a trick manual. Along with vet visits and trail rides, if you have a trained trick horse, you are going to be asked for a performance sooner or later. If your horse doesn't trailer, then you aren't going to get there. If you do manage to get there and your horse won't load, then you are going to lose all credibility - what kind of a trained trick horse won't even load into a trailer? Many times I have gone to horse shows and had 45 minutes worth of free entertainment because someone can't load his horse. These people try everything in the book. They try driving the horse in, luring the horse in, tricking him in, and forcing him in. Eventually, the horse gets bored and walks into the trailer and the people respond by slamming the door as fast as possible so that he can't 'escape'. Teach your horse to load properly and the show will be in the arena where it belongs, not in the back parking lot.

So, here we go! Start training at 9:00 in the morning (NO JOKE!!) and ensure that you have absolutely nothing else planned for the entire day. Once you start, you are going to see this through to the end - even if that end is 9:00 at night! Ensure that the trailer door is open and secure so that it doesn't slam shut at an inopportune time. Ensure that the trailer is securely attached to a truck so that the trailer doesn't roll or rock.

This is the concept that you are going to present to your horse: Outside the trailer is work, inside the trailer is rest and oats - same concept as was used on the pedestal. Get set up by putting the oats inside the trailer at the front. Put the water outside the trailer, somewhere out of the way.

Give your horse the benefit of the doubt and ask him to step up to the trailer. Let him smell around, and ask him to enter. If he doesn't enter, it's time to start longeing. Standing at the back of the trailer near the open door, ask your horse to longe. An easy trot is ok right now, as you are warming your horse up and introducing him to the whole concept of work vs. rest. After a few circuits on the longe line, stop your horse in front of the trailer door. You get in the trailer and ask your horse to "Step Up". Use Step Up as your verbal cue and it will come in handy every time you ask your horse to step up onto something. Be extremely aware of where your longe line is going. Don't let it wrap around your hands, arms, or legs. If your horse decides to haul backwards, you will get seriously hurt. Keep your longe line tidy at all times.

At this stage, he will probably only put his head in the trailer and smell the floor. This is just fine. As long as his head is in the trailer, give him a handful of oats, pet him, and let him relax. Step out of the trailer and continue on longeing. Stop in front of the trailer door and ask him to step up again. Now, you are going to have to start reading your horse. After 2 or 3 times of letting him just put his head in the door, start asking for more. If he shows any indication of forward movement, even just

148

leaning, then reward him. However, the more resistance he shows, the harder he works. If you ask him to come further into the trailer and instead he throws his head up and lunges backwards, then the time has come to start working him hard! No more leisurely trotting at the end of the longe line - get him moving fast. After three or four rotations, stop him in front of the trailer again and ask him to 'step up'. This time, don't settle for just a head in the trailer. You must always progress past the point where you last left off. If he progresses past the last point even a smidgen, then let him stand quietly and offer him a handful of oats. If he tosses his head and races backwards again, then return him to longeing fast. Repeat this process until he is standing quietly in the trailer. Don't get into a tug of war contest with him, you will lose. It takes absolutely no energy for a horse to lock up his legs and refuse to budge. If he does this, get him moving out on the longe line. He gets to rest in the trailer not in front of it - and a mule headed horse is just having a coffee break while you sweat bullets trying to budge him.

When your horse gets one foot (or even both front feet) in the trailer let him stand there for a few minutes. Pet him all over and tell him what a good boy he is. Let him stand quietly and eat a little bit of oats (not too much as he is probably pretty sweaty by now). Brush him, talk to him, and let him know that when he is in the trailer he gets to relax. Ask him to back out of the trailer and let him have a sip (just one sip mind you...you don't want your horse to colic!) of water. Walk back to the trailer and continue the loading lesson. Now your goal is to get all 4 feet in the trailer.

Now, how you get your horse out of the trailer is up to you. If it's a big trailer and backing out is never going to be an issue, then turn your horse around and let him walk out (just be prepared in case this decision comes back to haunt you). If you have a narrow trailer then you have no choice and backing out is what you have to do. Teaching a horse to back out of a trailer is all about being calm. He is going to be afraid of that big drop that he can't see behind him, so it's up to you to tell him when to step down. Ask your horse to back, and when appropriate, to step down. Expect him to sort of fall out of the trailer, then scare himself, and fly backwards the rest of the way. Don't scold him. Simply give him a second to gather his thoughts. Pat him and encourage him to be calm. Lead him around for a walk, then lead him back to the trailer. Get into the trailer and ask him to step up. If he gets in Hooray! If he refuses, it's back to the longe line. Once you get him in the trailer again, work on building his confidence in getting out. When he gets in and out of the trailer easily three times, you are done for the day and you can be confident that he will load easily.

Well, you might have noticed that the sections on Ground Rear and Trailer loading were suspiciously absent of pictures. Through pure luck, my sister, Joann, happened to be taking photos of Reamo during the training stages of his Riding Rear. Were it not for that, I wouldn't have any training photos of the Riding Rear either. Due to the nature of the liberty rear, very few horses that come my way, are taught it. The next one scheduled for the liberty rear is Duster...but that not for a while yet. I believe that I have detailed the liberty rear in such a way that you should still be able to train it...and by now, hopefully you have developed your own ideas on what will work best for you.

Regarding photos of Trailer Loading...when it came time to take these pictures, we discovered that there wasn't a horse on the place who didn't load perfectly!

NOTES:

These are just some musing that didn't fit anywhere else in this book.

I lived in Tokyo, Japan for a few months when I was 17 years old. Alone and away from my family, I decided to befriend a grubby dog that was chained a short distance from my apartment building. For weeks I would walk by this presumably white dog (he was so full of dirt and grease that he kind of came across as gray). I would say hello, bring it food…all to no avail. The dog hated me! He would bark his face off every time I came near. I was just at the point of thinking that the dog was untouchable when, one day, I saw a fellow sitting beside the dog talking to him – and the dog was turning himself inside out. Then, it struck me that I was in Japan! All this time I was speaking to the dog in English and the dog continually lost his mind. The next day, I walked up to the dog and greeted him with the local dialect of Konichiwa ("hello," in Japanese). Much to my delight, the dog started to wiggle and crawl on the ground in a classic happy-dog way. After that, the dog and I were solid friends. Due to my limited knowledge of Japanese, we didn't talk a lot but we had many good visits. The point I'm trying to make is, talk to your horses, they understand English! How would you like it if, everyday that you went to work, someone, without saying a word to you, would come and forcibly make your fingers work the keyboard on your computer? How about if they grabbed you by your head and, in utter silence, lead you to your office? It wouldn't be very enjoyable, would it? I know that we would all like to be able to talk to our horses on their level, but the truth is that we are humans. As humans, our natural tendency is to bring things into our world and our way of communicating. I think that the horse understands us way better then we will ever understand him. Talk to your horse like you would talk to a person and they just might start to 'talk' back to you.

When using praise as a reward, make sure that the inflection in your voice is such that your horse recognizes that he is being praised. Although difficult to describe on paper, imagine the difference in a monotone "step, step, step, good boy" compared to a highly energetic "step, step, step, GOOD BOY!". If you are verbally praising your horse, you have to do it from your heart. Even if your horse is being a brat, and you really don't think that he is a good boy at all, if he gives you what you are requesting, you have to put emotions and past screw-ups aside and make your verbal praise sound like you mean it.

After completing all or even some of the tasks in this book, you will probably start to realize that the relationship that you have with your horse has grown in depth and scale. If all of a sudden your horse stops performing, listen to what he is telling you. Perhaps his teeth hurt, or perhaps he has pulled a muscle. Before you start attacking your horse, give him the benefit of the doubt. I have once heard it said that "horses get headaches too." It would do us all well to remember this.

At the risk of never completing this book, I finally just had to send the darned thing to print. It seems as though one never finishes training a 'trick' horse since there is always room for improvement, refinement, and new ideas that come along. Once your horse can complete all the feats within this book, you might start to discover that the word 'trick' horse doesn't want to come off your tongue easily. The more I work with my horses, the more I dislike the descriptive terminology of 'trick' horse. A trick implies that there was sleight of hand and deception involved to complete trained feats. You are aware of the fact that these horses are the product of thousands of hours of hard work, training, and dedication. They are more than novelty animals in an exhibition sideshow, they are actors, performers, and trained athletes in their own right.

As the winter of 2003 begins to surrender to spring, I look forward to the summer when I can begin to explore a more eloquent form of 'trick' training. This summer I will start training my personal horses Obeisance (a more refined version of the stretching exercises), a combination of Obeisance and twisty legs, and lastly, hind leg walk. Lofty goals for a short Saskatchewan summer. My knowledge exhausted and published within this book, I look to the more experienced and senior members of the 'industry' to fill my brain and send me on new training paths. My mentors are the folks of the movie industry who have taken 'trick' horses to a higher level and produced stunt horses. There are also those who follow the training style of classical circus and exhibition riders, demonstrating movements and poses like levade, pesade, terre a terre and courbette.

As my dear friend John Knubben says: "In order to measure one's success as a horseman, one must measure one's self against one's peers."

I can only hope some day, to measure myself amongst some of these accomplished few.